The Claim

The Claim

A Mormon's Fight Against All Odds

A Novel

Rob Robles

Covenant Communications, Inc.

Published by Covenant Communications, Inc.
American Fork, Utah

Library of Congress Cataloging-in-Publication Data
ISBN 1-55503-744-5

The author would like to acknowledge certain individuals whose assistance was invaluable in the preparation of *The Claim*. Walter Hoppe and Dale Gillision provided wonderful insights into early Alta. Michael Rutter provided early editorial help. His encouragement and advice helped bring *The Claim* to publication.

PROLOGUE

Green spring grass carpeted the prairie and rolling hills. Willow buds were swollen, ready to explode. The violets and blues of wildflowers laced the creek bottoms. The sky was a deep blue, and puffy white clouds dotted the western horizon.

It had been three days since Bishop Spiers called me to herd cattle. I'd been dodging Jed Mathews ever since. Until now I'd been lucky—I'd been able to keep in sight of the wagons. But the cows had wandered behind a knoll, and I had to follow to keep them from getting lost in the thick willows that grew in the creek bottom.

Jed, on a dun gelding, rode out of the brush and spotted me. A fiendish glint came to his eyes. Putting his heels to his mount, he galloped toward me.

I was in the open, but not far from a thick hedge of rushes. I could have gotten away, but I wasn't going to run, even though Jed was four years older and a head taller. I wasn't afraid. A few weeks back I might have been more careful. Since the accident at the river I'd become hard on the inside. What could Jed do that would hurt more than losing Ma? I knew what was coming, but I didn't care.

Jed reined in and, kicking his leg over the horse's head, slid off his mount and stood in front of me. He was fifteen and beginning to show the muscles of a man. The wispy beginnings of a beard had started along his jawline. I'd heard the older girls whispering. They all liked his looks, but he was arrogant and a bully. Few of the older boys considered him a friend.

He pushed his hat back and spat on my boot. "Taw Stoner, you ain't been fair with me. The other boys with the herd have given me their ration of jerky. You been holding out," he sneered.

Without warning, he reached out and shoved me hard in the shoulder. I stumbled backward. He pressed forward, keeping in my face. "You don't want to get me upset, do you?"

He gave me another shove and pressed forward.

Several of the other boys came running when they saw Jed shove me. Now they stood back and watched, afraid to interfere. Bishop Spiers had called six of us to watch the spare oxen and cattle. Our job was to drive the herd away from the wagon trail, but in the same direction as the wagons. This allowed the cattle to feed on grass that hadn't been stomped into the ground by earlier wagon trains.

All of us were about the same age, except for Jed. An older boy was needed to keep us in line and, in case of trouble, to ride back to the wagons. Jed was always "yessiring" or "yes ma'aming" around the grownups. He'd sold Bishop Spiers on the notion that he was a good kid, just a might too playful at times. It wasn't until he was away from the wagons and grownups that the snake in him came out.

Being short on horses, all of us walked except for Jed. Jed's view of his job wasn't the same as the Bishop had described when he asked each of us to help. Jed tormented us endlessly. To keep us in tow, every time he could catch us away from the wagons he'd bully us and try to make us cry. He'd been able to corner all the other boys, but I'd kept myself scarce until now.

Jed pushed me again. I pushed back. Anger flashed in his eyes. He must have outweighed me by thirty pounds and stood nearly six inches taller. I'd been in my share of scrapes and had always been able to handle myself with boys my age. I had no hope against Jed though, but I didn't care.

Jed leaned forward pressing his face close to mine. "Taw! You're gonna . . ."

He never finished. I fired a roundhouse right into his mouth. His head snapped, and a look of astonishment spread across his face. I threw another right, but he blocked it with his arms. Then he slapped me so hard across the cheek that it made my knees buckle and spun me around.

Grabbing me by the back of the neck, he threw me down and ground my face into the dirt. He knelt on my back and pressed my face into the soft dirt. I gagged and choked. I couldn't get a breath of air. Beginning to panic, I tried to push myself up. But Jed just pushed all the harder. "This'll learn ya. If you ever try that again I'll grind you into the ground so far there won't even be a spot."

He jerked me to my feet and slapped me again. I stumbled backward. My cheeks were crimson. Scrapes covered my face. A tear slid down my dirty cheek. I trembled with hurt and fury. As long as I could stand I wasn't going to give in to him.

He stepped toward me again. I doubled up my fist. It was suicide, but I had to . . .

"Whoa . . . whoa . . . whoa!" Two horses carrying Bishop Spiers and my stepdad, Lars, charged up and slid to a stop. Obviously irritated, Bishop Spiers bellowed, "You boys stop this fighting. Jed, I'd better not hear about you fighting with one of these youngsters again. Catch that horse and make sure nothing strays off. You other boys get into those willows and don't let any cattle get bogged down."

Then, turning to me, the Bishop scolded, "Taw, clean yourself up. Don't let me catch you fighting again." It amazed me how a grownup could see such a one-sided thrashing and call it a fight.

Lars stepped off his wide-bodied draft horse. He gave me a stern look and in his Swedish accent said, "Taw, why can't you try to get along? Since your mother died you've been angry with the world. You can't go through your life this way, son."

I couldn't believe it. He was blaming me for the fight. I picked up my hat and turned, stomping toward the bullrushes.

Turning beet red, Lars shouted, "Don't you walk away from me."

I ignored him and ducked under a tangle of wispy willow shoots. I heard Lars cursing. Lars seldom swore. He was a pious man, but he had a fiery Swedish temper, and I had a way of bringing out the worst of it.

I continued into the willows and followed the creek. Lars' cursing faded in the distance. I found a fallen cottonwood and sat on the trunk. A cool trickle flowed at my feet. I untied the scarf from my neck and dipped it into the clear water.

I swabbed at the dirt and blood on my face. I winced with each wipe. Looking into a small pool, I saw a face covered with scrapes. The trickle of blood from my nose had slowed. I leaned back onto the log and gazed at the cottony clouds as they floated across the sky.

It had been two weeks since the river crossing. It seemed like two years. Bishop Spiers had spoken over Ma's grave, and I'd seen several men throw dirt on the blanket that covered her body. They'd dug the grave extra deep to keep wolves from uncovering her body. Then the men brushed out any trace of the grave, so Indians wouldn't find it. As we walked away, I turned back. Already I couldn't be sure of the exact spot where Ma was buried.

I couldn't get those pictures out of my mind. Why had this happened to Ma? Why did I have to be heading to a place I didn't want to go, and with a stepdad that didn't care? Why couldn't it have been someone else that drowned? Why couldn't it have been Lars? Why couldn't it have been . . . me?

I ached on the inside and nothing made it better. My sister Lucy was now my only kin. But how close can a guy be to a bossy older sister?

I was nearly a man and felt I shouldn't have had such feelings, but I missed Ma's hugs. I missed the way she kissed my forehead when she first saw me. After I was in bed she'd stroke my hair and hum a soft song she learned as a girl. I missed the way we'd talk and how she'd tell me about the things she'd done when she was a youngun. She could always get me to 'fess up about things that a boy ain't supposed to tell his ma, but she never got mad. She'd listen and let me know she understood. I had pretended to not like her singing, but how I missed it now! I would never hear her hum or feel her stroke my head. I'd never feel her hug, and I didn't have anybody to tell my secrets to.

My eyes were watering and I caught myself whispering, "Ma, why'd you have to die? If we hadn't come west. If you hadn't married Lars. If we'd never become Mormons . . . ."

That was it! If I'd known the pain that was in store, I'd have run those Elders off our place when I first saw them walking up our lane. That's what I should have done! Never let them in our yard. But all I could do now was sit and hopelessly wish it had all been just a bad dream.

Chapter One

The first time the Mormon missionaries wandered up our lane, I had just turned eleven and Lucy was sixteen. The war had come to an end, and a dollar was harder to find than whiskey at a Quaker picnic. I could tell they were preachers—preachers always carry their books different from other folks and seem to show up at supper time. They saw me milking and wandered over to the barn. The tall one spoke, "Boy, yer folks home?"

I should have lied. I pointed to the house. "Ma and my sister are inside."

They walked to the house. I saw them knock. Ma let them in.

Ma was the prettiest widow in the county. Pa had died years before. I was so young that I didn't remember him, but Ma said that with my light brown hair, dark brown eyes, and high cheek-bones that I must have looked like Pa when he was a boy.

Without a man around, the farm had gradually fallen into disrepair. Before the war we had the best place in the county. Four hundred acres of rich black dirt, plenty of water, and the best farming tools made. But when all the men marched off to join the fight, Ma couldn't find help. She had to give up farming most of the bottomland, and she had to sell the milk cows because we couldn't keep up. With so little money coming in, she had to sell off bits and pieces of the farm along with our fancy carriages and furniture. We were left with the farm house, the barn, forty acres, and enough cows and pigs to keep us fed.

After a spell Ma hollered. As I wiped of my feet each of the men told me their names. The taller man, Elder Stoll, was older than Ma, and had kind blue eyes. But eyes were the only thing worth looking at. He had no teeth in front, and his face was covered with terrible scars. Part of his head didn't have any hair, and his right ear was missing.

I found out later that Elder Stoll had been burned badly while working for the railroad. While filling several lanterns at the depot, he dropped a lighted lantern on the table with the other lanterns. Burning oil splattered into his hair and beard. He went up like a human torch. Flames leapt several feet into the air as he stumbled outside and rolled in the dirt. None of the people who saw him thought he'd live. Day after day he laid in bed, screaming with pain—but refusing to die. Members of his church prayed over him, and one month later he started working again.

The other man, Elder Scott, was shorter, husky, and about marrying age. I thought it strange that they both had the same first name. With short arms and short legs, Elder Scott looked like he should be called "Stump." His eyes were light blue and his hair blonde. He spoke real polite. He must have had a ma that didn't put up with backtalk. Like all the boys in town, his eyes followed Lucy wherever she went.

All the local boys were in love with Lucy. She was tall with long dark hair and dark brown eyes. People said she was as pretty as Ma and that they looked so much alike they could be sisters. I didn't think so. The last few years Lucy had been going to some fancy girls' school in Philadelphia. Ma said it was to teach her proper and help her become a lady. All it seemed to do was to help her put on airs and make her more bossy. The missionaries talked to Ma and Lucy about a man named Joseph Smith who received some gold bible from an angel. They carried several copies of the gold bible. Ma and Lucy were impressed with their story. The two men stayed for supper, and Ma bought one of their books. Elder Stoll invited Ma to go to one of their meetings in town on the next Sunday. Ma said she'd try.

As the preachers rose to leave, Elder Stoll turned and said that what he taught us was the truth and if we'd pray about it we'd know for our ownselves. While he spoke I felt something. I couldn't explain it, but it was nice. I didn't know what it was, but I'd never felt that way before. I looked over and Lucy was crying. The two men waved, ducked outside and walked down the road. Later that night as I laid in my bed, my head was troubled with what I'd felt. Did Elder Stoll tell the truth? Would I get an answer if I prayed? I fell asleep wondering. The next morning I got busy with chores and didn't give it any more mind.

I never expected to see those preachers again. Ma got busy during the week, and when Sunday came around we went to our normal Sunday meeting, not to Elder Stoll's. It surprised me when, two days after Sunday, Elder Scott and another man named Elder Samuelson stopped by. I decided right then I wasn't going to any church that made me change my name. They taught us again and got Ma and Lucy to promise to read out of the their bible. Ma and Lucy kept their promise, and two weeks later Elder Scott and Elder Samuelson visited us once more.

During the preachers' next visit, I found out that they had ordinary names. Elder was a type of nickname. That made me feel a lot better. I also found out they called themselves Mormons. Elder Samuelson asked Ma for permission to hold a meeting in our house Sunday evening. Ma rolled her eyes, but finally agreed. Elder Scott never said much—he just looked at Lucy.

Ma had always been a churchgoing person. She made me go to church every Sunday. It didn't even matter if the fish were biting. Lucy or Ma usually read from the Bible every night. But these Mormons really got her fired up. She talked about their gold bible, and whenever the two Elders came by she wore out her jaw asking questions.

Ma and Lucy were like a couple of hummingbirds, zipping around our house getting ready for the meeting. They even made me shovel the stalls and pull the weeds around the house. This on top of the normal wood to chop and cows to milk! I hoped those Elders didn't make a habit of holding their meetings here. Ma couldn't keep what she learned to herself, so the night of the meeting she invited several of the neighbors.

I was dreading that meeting almost as much as I dreaded kissing my Aunt Sadie, the one with hog bristles above her upper lip. I got blisters from hauling water so everybody could take a bath. Ma made me wear my new wool shirt and pants, which had me dripping sweat. The shirt was not only hot, but it made me itch like I had the chicken pox. Ma borrowed a new pair of shoes from one of the neighbors, but they were a couple sizes too small. They hurt so bad I had to grit my teeth to keep the tears from flowing.

About half past four in the afternoon, sweaty, itchy, and limping, I greeted folks and put up their teams. Everyone was "Brother this" or "Sister that." Elder Scott, Elder Samuelson, and Elder Stoll were there along with an Elder Whitney. He looked like one of them bankers that used to call on Ma. He had grey hair and large bushy sideburns. He was slender, average in height, and had dark brown eyes. He wore a fancy suit. He was one of the friendliest people I'd ever met. When he came over and spoke to me, it seemed he knew me all of his life.

As the time approached for the meeting to start, I dreaded what I expected to happen. I'd sat through revival meetings and knew what to expect. The head preacher would walk back and forth, pointing his finger and yelling to raise the dead. He'd call us sinners and tell us we were all going to burn up in hell. After lots of hallelujahs and a couple of hymns, he'd ask for money and everyone would go home.

As the music started for the first hymn, I slipped off my

shoes and prepared for an evening of itchy misery. After the hymn Elder Stoll stood up. No one seemed to notice the terrible burn scars on his face. He offered a short prayer, thanking the Lord for his many blessings! My mouth fell open. He had looks that would make a baby cry and he considered himself lucky?

Elder Whitney stood up and began speaking. But he didn't talk like any preacher I ever heard before. He didn't yell or scream, he didn't tell us we were all sinners, and he didn't ask for money. He talked about the Book of Mormon. He talked about Joseph Smith and how an angel gave him the gold plates. He also talked about Jesus. He looked at us as if his eyes were on fire, and when he looked at me it seemed as if his eyes looked right through me. I had that same strange, kind of warm feeling I'd had the first time Elder Stoll met with us. Elder Whitney turned to Ma and Lucy and asked them if they'd be baptized. Ma and Lucy didn't hesitate—they said yes.

A few days later Ma, Lucy, and me, along with about twenty other people, met at the pond behind the Harrison place. In all the excitement, no one got around to asking me what I thought about being baptized. I had felt something when the Elders were around, but I didn't know what. Was that how prayers were answered? I didn't know and I didn't know why we had to be baptized. But Ma had her mind set and if I complained I'd have probably got a few whacks with a hickory. Rather than cause problems I went along.

Elder Stoll and Elder Samuelson did the baptizing and at the end of the ceremony a picnic lunch was spread out on the grass near the pond. Elder Scott hung blankets so all the men and women could change out of their wet clothes. We sat next to a big Swede by the name of Lars Swensen. He, along with his older children, had also been baptized. He was a widower with five young blond-haired, blue-eyed kids who all looked the same. I learned that his wife had died when the youngest was born.

Brother Swensen and Ma talked all afternoon. He told all kinds of stories about his life and his kids. He had worked as a teamster, hauling freight in heavy wagons he built himself. He never knew where his next job would be so he had to keep moving.

He had come to America when he was fifteen as a member of a ship's crew. The company owning the ship he worked on went broke while it was docked in Boston Harbor, so Brother Swensen decided to stay in America. He married, and after having a mob of kids, his wife died. After she died he bought a small place and became a farmer so he wouldn't have to chase work. I couldn't understand what Ma found so interesting. His stories bored me to death.

He had arms and shoulders bigger than most men I'd seen. His loud voice and booming laugh could be heard above all the others. Late in the afternoon Ma and Lucy rode back in his wagon while I led their horses. Our carriage had broke an axle several months before, and Ma didn't have the money to repair it. Brother Swensen noticed, and two days later he dropped by and fixed it. With no grown man around and no money, all sorts of things were busted. So, over the next couple of months Brother Swensen made himself mighty handy.

Bankers from Philadelphia were always calling on Ma. Some carried canes and had handshakes like wet sponges. They'd sit on the porch and try to put on airs. Then Brother Swensen would show up in his big heavy wagon and his matching pair of old mules. His clothes were dusty from the day's work, and when he climbed down off the wagon and shook my hand it felt like my eyeballs were going to pop out. He wasn't one for talking much. He just waved to Ma and went to work mending a broken fence or a busted corral gate. When he finished he waved good-bye and jogged the mules down the lane.

No matter what broke, Brother Swensen fixed it. He usually brought a couple of his half-wild kids along. Those kids were like a pack of mad dogs screaming around our yard. But Ma really appreciated the work. The other gentlemen who visited Ma never offered to help. They didn't seem to take to hard work. Over the months Ma began to look forward to Brother

Swensen's visits. He arrived, did whatever work needed to be done, and never asked for nothing.

Then one day, Ma and Brother Swensen hit us with a real surprise. They were going to get hitched! I didn't even know they'd been courting! I didn't know what to think, but Lucy was bellowing like a bull on the prod. She wanted Ma to marry one of those bankers. But Ma said she loved Lars and he would make her happy.

A couple weeks later they married, and I became a big brother to a bunch of blond-haired, blue-eyed demons. I found myself sharing my bed with my new younger brother, Paul. Brother Swensen became Papa Swensen, though I could never call him that. I called him Lars.

With all of these strangers in the family, life changed a lot. Kids screamed through the house and were always causing trouble. If I played hookey from school, some younger brother or sister made sure Ma knew. If they weren't pulling on the dog's ears they were trying to ride one of the weaner pigs. Snakes appeared in the milk bucket, pine cones found their way into my bed, and bows decorated the horse's tail.

Other things began to change, too. Word got out that we were Mormons. The Jameses down the road a piece, who'd been our friends for years, wouldn't talk to us anymore. I'd always gotten into my share of trouble at school, but now I was getting into a fight almost everyday. The older boys constantly picked on me. But even though they were a year older, I never backed down and dished out my share of lumps.

The worst part was that the schoolmarm seemed to have it in for me, too. She'd catch me and some older boy rolling in the dirt and I'd be the one who got the knuckle cracker. That's when I first began to think that being a Mormon wasn't such a good idea. But Ma and Lars were devoted to their new religion. We all read from the Book of Mormon most every night, and prayers were very important. Lars always carried his Book of Mormon with him and managed to work in a story from it whenever he spoke.

I guess I didn't have the makings to be good at religion. All this bible reading and praying didn't set with me. Lars would begin a prayer and a stampede of horses with a dozen wild Indians chasing could run through the house and he'd just keep going. Sometimes he'd pray so long that the taters got cold. I hated to see that happen to good food, so when everybody's eyes were closed I'd sneak a bite, but Lucy always peeked.

If I wasn't in trouble for sneaking food I got in trouble for fidgeting. I couldn't help it. I'd get an itch somewhere and just about die waiting for the prayer to end.

When it was my turn, I'd make up for Lars' long-winded prayers. With a thank you and good-bye, my prayer would be over before Lars cleared his throat. Ma got after me and told me I should be more thoughtful, but I never seemed to get it right.

When all my old friends stopped talking to me, I wound up spending my time with my stepbrother, Paul. Paul was a year and a half younger than me. Like all the Swensens, he had blond hair and blue eyes. He was built like his pa—a brick with legs. Paul didn't seem to have the same problems with being a Mormon that I did. He never got into fights at school, and the marm liked him because he knew all the answers. He didn't seem to mind when Lars was blessing every person in the county. When it was his turn to pray, he always said it just right. I liked him okay. In fact, he was my only friend.

Time passed, and I tried to accept my new life and Ma's new religion. Then Ma gave me another surprise. She and Lars decided the family would move to the Valley of the Salt Lake with the rest of the Saints. I didn't think about it at the time, but later I figured Lars must have talked her into it.

Lucy declared war. Going to that fancy school had spoiled her, and she had come to expect she would marry the son of some wealthy lawyer. When Lucy talked to Ma about the move, she hollered loud and long. But, after many tears and words, she decided to come with us to the Valley of the Great Salt Lake.

Chapter Two

Early the next spring, we started our journey to the Valley of the Salt Lake. After selling both farms and our animals, we rode the train to St. Joseph, Missouri, and caught a river boat to the town of Wyoming, Nebraska. We joined a large group of Mormons, mostly from Germany and England. The Mormons in Salt Lake sent over forty wagons with teams of oxen or mules for those who didn't have any. An immigrant family could use a wagon and team, but were expected to haul a thousand pounds of freight in return. The money from the sale of our farms made us better off than most of the other Saints, so we were able to buy two wagons, extra stock, and supplies. Since we owned our own wagons and teams, Lars carried extra supplies we could use in Salt Lake. In a cold rain in early April, we set out with almost four hundred people.

The trip to the river crossing at Ft. Kearney was horrible. Almost every day we walked in a heavy, freezing rain. The days were blurs of pushing and pulling the wagons through heavy mud. After a wagon would mire down in the deep mud, we'd hitch both teams to the front. After freeing it, we would then hitch both teams to the other wagon and start all over again. Lars would use a long pole and pry the wheels free while Ma guided the teams. Me and Paul would lay branches or logs in front of the wagon wheels to keep them from sinking. But mostly we got hollered at. Lucy stayed in one of the wagons and kept the younguns in line, but she came down with scarlet fever and Ma feared she might not make it. This left the younguns to watch themselves, and it didn't work very well.

Those first few weeks were the longest of my life. We made so little progress! If I'd been given a say I'd have turned back, but Lars and Ma weren't bothered. They were going to Salt Lake if it killed us all. There were times I thought it might.

Most nights we were so exhausted that we ate supper and dropped into our blankets to sleep like dead men—except for Ma, who stayed up each night drying our muddy clothes over the fire. Before daylight, Lars roused us awake and we began all over again.

After two weeks, we reached the crossing on the Platte River, but we couldn't cross. Mormon companies always traveled on the north side, the gentiles on the south. Many in the gentile trains claimed to have been with the mobs in Missouri that had attacked Mormons years earlier. Brigham Young felt it wisest to keep the Saints separate from the gentile trains.

Ft. Kearney was the only place to cross the Platte at this time of year because the fort operated a ferry. But the river was so high that the ferry wasn't running. We camped five days waiting for the river to drop.

The high waters had washed away the sandbar that the ferry usually started from and had cut away a large part of the bank. It left us with no way down to the river from the thirty-foot bluff. The men got busy and soon cut a steep ramp down to the ferry landing. The ramp was not much wider than the wagons and so steep that a man would have to ride the brake lever all the way down. With luck and a prayer the wagon wouldn't slide off the edge and into the rushing waters of the Platte.

To descend to the river a driver drove his wagon to the head of the ramp. Two men on horseback tied their catch ropes to the back of the wagon and dallied the loose end around their saddle horn to help slow the wagon.

As each wagon started down, the driver would lean into his brake lever and hold back his oxen, and the two riders behind the wagon would lean their horses into the ropes. Oxes bellowed, men hollered, and somehow none of the wagons slid into the river.

At the bottom, the team pulled the loaded wagon onto the barge. Three yoke of oxen were attached to a long rope tied to the far end of the barge. Another rope was tied across the river to help the raft across. When the raft was ready to leave, the ferry operator blew a horn and the man across the river started his teams to pulling the heavy rope attached to the raft. Only one large wagon could fit on the barge, so the process of ferrying the entire company across the river would take several days.

I watched for half a day before our turn came. Lars, being in his usual hurry, shouted, "Younguns get inside with Lucy. Men, secure your catch ropes. Paul and Taw, make yourselves handy."

The first of our two wagons carried the children and food. Paul and I did what we could to help, but nothing we did made Lars happy. His impatience made the crossing miserable.

After we loaded all the younguns and made sure everything was tied down, Lars steered our wagon into place. When everyone was ready he started the wagon down. He hollered, "You boys stand to the side and keep out of the way."

The wagon started down the steep ramp. About half-way down the ramp a long crack appeared in the dirt wall where the ramp met the cut bank. The ramp had been dug in the side of a bluff that started about thirty feet above the river. A wagon going down would have one wheel touching the dirt wall and the other wheel inches from falling off the edge. A crack appeared where the angled road met the dirt wall. As the wagon started down, the crack seemed to widen, hinting that the ramp was about to break away and fall into the river. The day-long traffic and misting rain had made the incline treacherous. It was wet, muddy and as slippery as ice on a stone floor. The oxen strained and bellowed clouds of vapor as they fought to slow the wagon's descent.

Lars leaned on the wagon brake with all his strength, but the wheels locked and slid down the slippery surface. The men on horseback were literally dragged down the mucky trail. The horses couldn't keep their footing and slid along the muddy surface. The men couldn't control the wagon. They shouted for help, and several others threw ropes on the wagon to gain control. Lars struggled with the reigns while leaning on the brake lever, the veins on his neck popping out. Above him, I frantically yelled, "The bank's about to give way!"

Lars didn't hear. His attention was focused on keeping the big wagon and team from plunging into the muddy brown Platte.

The wagon skidded to the bottom of the ramp and stopped before sliding into the water. The bellowing oxen pulled the wagon onto the ferry as the intensity of the rain increased. Soaking wet and ornery as a bear after a long winter, Lars came stomping up the slimy hill with fire in his eyes. He looked at us, "Be quick about it. Get on the ferry."

I started, "Lars, you have to . . . ."

He cut me off, bellowing, "Didn't I tell you to get on the raft?" He turned back to help with the second wagon.

I ran to him, grabbing him by the sleeve. "You have to . . . ."

He spun, fire in his eyes. "Board!"

The ferry operator rang his bell. Paul begged, "You're looking for a whuppin. Let's get on the raft." His hand was on my shoulder, but I pulled away.

Icy rain began falling in sheets. The river was rising noticeably. If the river continued to rise, the ferry operator would stop taking wagons across.

Lars was in a fix. One wagon with all the kids and food was about to leave for the north side of the river. The river was rising quickly, and if he didn't get the second wagon across quickly, he and Ma could be separated from the kids and food for days until the river dropped again.

I ran to him as he moved the second wagon to the top of the

ramp. "Lars, you have to listen to me. There's . . . ."

"Taw!" He cut me off. He pointed a finger at the raft. Then he turned his back. His face was beet red. I dared not push him any more. He'd never whupped me, but I knew he had it in him. I turned and ran down the mucky ramp and jumped onto the ferry as it pulled away from shore.

I turned and watched the men as they prepared the wagon for the descent. The men had decided to use an ox team at the back of the wagon because they were stronger than the horses. Lars climbed down in the mud and attempted to hook up the team to the wagon. Ma had stayed inside the wagon with Lucy. Lucy's fever had not improved, so Ma refused to allow her to even walk down the hill to the other wagon. A couple of horses took the place of the oxen in the front of the wagon and started the descent, while the ox team was placed in the rear to keep the wagon from descending too rapidly.

The wagon started down. The ferry was about fifty feet from shore. As I watched I could tell that something was wrong. I saw the corner of the wagon begin to sag, and suddenly I realized what was happening. The whole section of bank began to give way, and the wagon started to slide toward the muddy, rolling Platte. I heard several men shout and jump away from the wagon. The horses screamed in terror and frantically thrust themselves against their harnesses. The wagon began to tip and slide sideways as the entire section of dirt bank fell into the brown water. The men hanging onto ropes tried to halt the fall, but their efforts proved useless.

I stood frozen and watched the wagon crash sideways into the frigid brown water. The two horses still harnessed to the wagon made a huge splash as they plunged, frantically flailing their legs. A cascade of mud and dirt thundered down on the wagon, pushing it under like a coffin.

Several men who had been holding the wagon were pulled into the water. All that was visible of the overturned wagon was one wheel sticking up from below the surface. I tried to jump in to swim to the wagon. The bulky operator grabbed me in his huge arms and held me. I fought like a wildcat. I screamed for Ma.

Some of the men were trying to save themselves, while others were trying to get inside the wagon. As the ferry moved away, it got hard to see what was happening. As we neared the far bank, I stopped struggling and gave in to a series of uncontrollable sobs.

Chapter Three

I staggered as the ferry bumped into the dock. I was in a daze. Had the wagon really fallen into the river, or was it a dream? Brother Hutchings jumped aboard the ferry. He had seen the wagon fall into the water from this side of the river. He begged the ferry captain to take us back across.

"The current's so strong that we nearly didn't make it this time. Those ropes wouldn't have held if it had taken us a minute longer," the ferry captain stated, pointing to the guide ropes. "I ain't in no hurry to meet my Maker. I'd give ya even money that the ferry would break loose if we tried again now. Once ya break loose, ya might as well start planning the funeral. Ya got no hope against them rocks down river."

The ferry captain walked over to me and put his hand on my shoulder. "Boy," he said, "I know how ya feel. Don't ya see that there's nothing ya can do to help yer folks back on the other side? It ain't worth risking yer life. We'll have to wait until the river drops and it's safe."

The ferry captain turned and led the team off the ferry.

My hope persisted that Ma and Lucy had survived, but deep down I couldn't believe it was possible. What was I going to do if they hadn't made it? The thought started the tears to flowing again.

I didn't know if Lars fell into the water, but every time I thought of him, I was filled with a sense of loathing. It wouldn't have happened if he'd have listened.

Sister Hutchings and her husband took the children to her wagon where she prepared a hot meal. I couldn't take myself away from the ferry dock. I had to know what happened, yet there was no way across. After a while Paul walked to me. He was angry with his father, too. He put his arm on my shoulder.

"My pa done a fool thing. He should have let you say your piece. But he loved your ma . . . ."

I snorted and brushed his arm aside.

Tears welled in Paul's eyes. His lip quivered. "Pa's a good man. He loved your ma. He'd never hurt her. If there was any way to save your ma, Pa would die trying." Paul's voice cracked. Then he turned and ran off.

I felt a lump in my throat. Brother Hutchings walked up and said, "You come and join us in a prayer for those that fell in the water."

During the prayer I wondered, *What good is this doing? Didn't we have a prayer this morning? Look what happened.*

I couldn't stand it. I jumped up in the middle of the prayer and ran to the ferry dock. With tears in my eyes, I looked over the rolling Platte and swore a silent oath. If Ma didn't make it, I'd never pray again. I thought the night would never end. I hoped, but deep down I didn't believe I'd see her again. The next day dawned sunny and clear. The river had dropped half a foot in the night. Down at the ferry dock there was a big argument.

Brother Hutchings demanded, "You've got to take us across. This boy's kin were in the wagon that fell in the river. He's got to know what happened."

The ferry operator was picking his teeth with his sheath knife. "Can't do that. River's still too high," he drawled.

They haggled back and forth for a spell. Finally Brother Hutchings got tired. "Get out of the way, because we're taking the ferry whether you come or not."

The ferry operator scratched his huge belly. "All right. Jest you and the boy. Too dangerous for any more." Then, softening, he said, "Reckon if it was my folks I'd feel the same."

As we neared the shore, I saw several lines tied from the bank to the wagon, laying on its side under water. A dead horse had washed up on the muddy bank fifty feet downstream. Two wagon wheels were all that could be seen of the sunken wagon. Folks were gathered at the launch. I looked everywhere, but neither Ma nor Lucy was in the crowd.

When the ferry docked, I ran to the group and cried out, "What happened to Ma?" Their look told me. I fell down, but there were no more tears left. I sat in silence, dropping my head into my hands and staring at the ground. A heavy woman, Sister Spiers, approached and standing above me said, "Boy, your mother drowned . . . but your sister made it. She's in the large wagon near the fire at the top of the hill."

My heart leaped. Lucy!

As I hurried up the ramp to the wagon, Sister Spiers told me what happened. As the wagon began to slide into the river, Ma grabbed Lucy and shoved her out the back. She fell free of the wagon and one of the men on the stream bank jumped in when he saw her struggling. As the wagon hit the main current, a mountain of mud and debris trapped Ma inside. Several men tried to free her, but by the time they reached her, she had drowned.

Lucy appeared near death. The time spent in the freezing water had made her even sicker. Some whispered that she wouldn't make it. I caught a glimpse of her lying amid a bunch of quilts—her sickly gray face met my gaze. Sister Spiers pulled me aside. "It ain't good news for your sister. If the fever don't break soon, she won't make it."

Lars, Bishop Spiers, and two others prepared to give Lucy a blessing. I didn't want Lars to have anything to do with my sister. Hadn't he done enough already? Somebody said a prayer, and then Lars and the other men put their hands on her head. Lars cleared his throat and blessed her.

"Lucy," he said, "you've been through a terrible experience. But you need to know that the Lord knows your ma was a wonderful woman. She blessed every life she touched. Now she's been called to another part of his vineyard. There are others that need the special love that only she can give. As much as you are going to miss her, you need to know that she is happy and one day will see you again, if you remain worthy. I bless you with a full and rapid recovery." Then he ended the blessing.

I wanted to believe, but my feelings about Lars wouldn't let me. He said "Amen," and everyone climbed out of the wagon. As I walked away, Lars approached and stood in front of me. His large, broad frame blotted out the sun. I looked up into his tear-streaked face. Dirt smeared his cheeks where he had wiped the tears away with a dirty hand. Putting a hand on my shoulder, he said, "Taw, I know how you must feel about your ma."

I replied, "You don't know nothing! If you'd listened, none of this would have happened!"

He gave me a questioning look and asked, "What are you talking about?"

"I saw cracks!" I shouted. "It looked like the ramp would break away. I tried to tell, but you wouldn't listen!"

He looked at me in silence. He wiped his face and, shaking his head, kneeled down so he could look me directly in the eyes. He grabbed me tightly by one shoulder and looked off in the distance for a long time. Then he whispered to me, "What have I done? What have I DONE?" He choked up and dropped his head, trying to hide the tears.

"Can you forgive me? I didn't know." He paused. "I should have listened."

I tried to pull away, but he tightened his iron grip on my shoulder. He said, "Son, I know you're blaming me right now, and I probably deserve the blame. But you're not the only one who loved your ma. She was a special woman, and in the short time I spent with her, she brought me more happiness than I've known in years."

I looked into his eyes. Lars tried to pull me close. I pulled away. I don't know why. At that moment, I wanted more than anything to call him Pa and hug him, but I couldn't. He looked at me with saddened eyes, then stood up and slowly walked away. He picked up a shovel to do one more thing—bury Ma.

The next day Lucy's fever broke, the sun dried the mud, and larks filled the meadows with their song. The rest of the wagons crossed the river, and our journey west began.

Chapter Four

Three days after crossing the Platte, the wagon train stopped for a day. The men unloaded plows and plowed a flat field while the women and children followed, sowing wheat in the freshly tilled earth. It seemed crazy to me. Why waste a day this way? I found out we were planting grain so later Mormon wagon trains could harvest it. Little did I know how thankful I would be when a couple of months later, with supplies almost gone, we crested a rise and found a field of golden wheat waiting for us to harvest.

The next couple of weeks I didn't want to see anyone. I drove one of the wagons and didn't talk. When camped, if Lars came near I'd turn and walk away. He decided to let me be.

After two weeks, Bishop Spiers figured I'd mourned enough and called me aside. "Taw, I'm calling you to help herd the spare cattle. They need to be kept strong. So you, Paul, and several others will drive them on fresh grass in the same direction the wagons are heading. Any trouble and you get back to the wagons immediately."

"It's time you stop grieving your ma. There ain't a body on this train that hasn't lost a loved one to accident or sickness. Mourning ain't going to do any good. You got to concern yourself with the living. The deceased will take care of themselves."

He turned to walk away. "By the way, I put Jed Mathews in charge of you boys." He continued back to the wagons.

The idea of spending the day away from the wagons excited me. But I hadn't met Jed yet. That was going to change real soon.

That's how I became a Mormon, and that's how Lars became my stepdad. Now I'm heading to the Valley of the Great Salt Lake, and I've got to always look over my shoulder for Jed.

Later in the day of my fight with Jed, he caught up with me, Paul, and the Duncan brothers in a willow thicket. He threatened, "I'm in charge when we're away from the wagons. Any of you get the least uppity or tell your folks what's happened, and I'll make you pay. As long as you got a ration of jerky, it's mine. Lest you want to end up looking like Taw."

He put his spurs to his gelding and galloped away. We all hated him, but there was nothing we could do. The first few weeks after crossing the Platte we had plenty of fresh meat. Prairie chickens, turkeys, and antelope were everywhere. Then one day all the wild game disappeared. Several parties of men rode out to hunt. They didn't even find a track. We couldn't risk killing stock for meat, since we'd need them once we arrived in the valley.

A month later, with nothing but flour and water gruel, I had such a craving for meat that I'd eaten my fingernails down to the quick.

Late one afternoon we came across an old, abandoned corral. The corral sat in a marshy spot near good grass. A quarter mile away a spring bubbled from the ground. Inside the corral, the scrawniest looking ox I ever saw stood with glazed eyes. He was nothing but gray hide stretched over sharp bones. An earlier train apparently left him and didn't want to waste the ammunition to put him out of his misery. A few thought of butchering him, but upon a closer look, the animal didn't have enough meat to make the effort worthwhile.

Jed overheard the men talking. He reasoned there might not be enough for the whole train, but enough could be scraped from the bones to feed one or two families. He figured to sneak out at night, butcher the ox, and return without anyone knowing. He needed help, and that is where Paul and me fit in.

That evening Jed rode up to Paul and me as we were driving the last of the stock to the wagons. He jumped off his horse and stood in front of me. "What do you want, Jed?" I asked.

"That ox back in the corral. There's not enough meat on him to split between all the families on the trail, but I think enough could be scraped from his bones to make a meal or two. I'm going to slaughter him tonight. I need help."

"Good. Go find someone else," I answered. Paul nervously stood off to the side, not speaking.

"You don't get it. You two are going to help me tonight," he threatened.

"No we're not. Find some . . . " I never finished.

Jed grabbed me by the front of my shirt. "Stoner, you and Paul will meet near that old dead snag after dark. Be there . . . or else."

I could fight him, but I'd come out the worst of it. It would be a lot less painful to go along with him. But I wasn't going to let him best me. "We get half the meat or we're not coming."

"All right, you get half the meat. Don't be late." He turned and walked away.

We met him after dark. He was carrying a catch rope and said he'd borrowed a knife. As we walked along the trail, he explained his plan. "Butchering the ox shouldn't be difficult. It's nearly dead. It couldn't put up much of a fight." He continued his blabbering, "I can't wait. Hot stew with juicy chunks of meat. The first in a month." That got my mouth watering.

Jed described his plan. It was simple enough. We'd throw a rope around the ox's neck and cinch him to a corral post. Jed would cut his throat, we'd skin him, and take whatever meat we found. I didn't see how anything could go wrong.

Several hours later, we still hadn't found the ox. Jed had failed to notice that the corral gate was open when he looked at the ox earlier in the day. I was tired and footsore. I wanted to sleep, but Jed insisted upon searching for the ox.

We stumbled around some more and finally spotted the ox grazing in a marshy hollow. As we approached, the ox became more lively than we expected.

The beast knew this was a party he didn't want to attend. As Jed sneaked near to throw his rope, the ox walked into the marsh. We did our best to follow, but with each step we sank over our boot tops in the mud. The ox could travel easier and stayed out of reach.

We slogged our way out of the mess and sat down on the grass to make up a new plan. Paul whined, "I'm too tired. I want to go back."

Paul's vote didn't count. Jed's slug to the shoulder let him know that.

I argued, "We're going to run more meat off our bones than we'll ever get from the ox. Let's go back."

Jed got all huffed up and strutted over to me. It didn't take many guesses to figure what he planned to do. I was too tired and cold to care. He grabbed me and we wrestled for a minute. Then he got me in a headlock. He must have figured he had me under control, because he began explaining how we were going to rope the ox.

It was the craziest plan I had ever heard, but I wasn't in a position to argue. "You're going to climb that old tree with one long, low branch. Me and Paul will drive the ox under you. You drop out of the tree and wrap your arms around his neck. You hold him the best you can. I'll be nearby and put the rope around his head while you're wrestling with him."

"I got a better idea. You climb the tree." Jed didn't like my plan and thumped me in the head in answer.

While Jed had me in the headlock working out the plan, Paul sneaked away. When Jed let me go, Paul was gone. We searched for a while, with Jed cursing all the time.

We heard a yell. We scampered back to the marsh and saw Paul with both arms around the neck of the animal. The ox was dragging him all around the field. Jed gave chase, hollering, "Don't let go!"

In the moonlight, I could see Paul's eyes wide with terror.

Jed tried to keep up and get the rope over the ox's head, but Paul's arms were in the way. Jed had to be satisfied with the catch rope around the horns.

Snugging the rope, Jed shouted and Paul let go, falling away and breathlessly jumping to his feet. "I . . . I got so tired I couldn't hold my eyes open," he explained. "I sneaked over to a dry grassy spot and laid down. That fool ox walked over and laid down next to me. I knew if I yelled he'd get up and run, so I jumped aboard and held on."

The ox, exhausted from its ordeal, tugged for a moment on the rope, but then lay down in the grass as if waiting for its fate. We needed to cinch the rope to something so Jed could cut its throat. There were no trees in the field, and we couldn't budge the ox.

Jed came up with a new plan. Jed and Paul were going to hold the ox's head down while I used the knife. The thought passed through my mind that I should use the knife on someone other than the ox, but it didn't stay long. Jed brought out the knife. He hadn't bothered to tell us that he couldn't sneak his pa's good hunting knife, so he brought a rusted old blade that someone found on the trail.

The knife had obviously been lost from an earlier wagon train and probably spent the winter in the mud. It was a mass of rust—no one had gotten around to putting an edge on it. I waved the knife in Jed's face. "This'll never cut through his tough neck hide. Our only hope is that he sees it and worries himself to death."

Jed sneered, "Get to work or I'll use that knife on you."

While Paul and Jed pulled the rope taut, I straddled that old ox and tried to cut through its neck hide. The ox didn't seem to notice my efforts. His hide was so tough I think he did more damage to the knife than it did to him.

Finally I drew blood and got his attention. He gave a loud snort, got up angrily, and sent me flying, only to find himself in a tug-o-war with Paul and Jed. Jed was cursing and shouting at me, "Use the knife, use the knife!"

Every time I got near him, the ox shook his big old head and knocked me flying. The half-dead ox had come to life like Lazarus in the Bible. He shook off Jed, but Paul froze and wouldn't let go. The ox decided he had had enough of this nonsense and bolted toward the marsh. Paul found himself bouncing through the smelly mud of the marsh on the end of the rope. The rope slipped from Paul's hand and the ox disappeared into the heavy willows nearby.

Paul staggered out of the marsh covered in putrid mud. I could hardly keep from falling down with laughter, but Jed's shrieking soon brought me to my senses. "My pa's catch rope. You lost his rope. We've got to find it!"

Jed realized the trouble he faced if he lost the catch rope. There were no other ropes available on the train and no spare hides to make one. Paul rolled in the grass and tried to wipe himself off while Jed stood above, threatening to skin both of us for losing his rope. Exhausted, sore, and muddy, we started looking for the ox again.

We crawled through every briar and willow patch in the creek bottom. After several hours, I told Jed I didn't care what happened, Paul and me were going back to the wagons. Jed, very discouraged, agreed. He joined us as we tramped back to camp.

To my amazement, as we approached the corral, the ox stood in the center with the rope hanging from his horns. With renewed vigor, we secured the gate. Jed sauntered up, grabbed the rope, and walked the ox to a large post, where he cinched it and quickly cut its throat with the rusty knife.

The hard work began. We sawed and hacked on that ox carcass. Jed and I took turns with the knife because Paul kept falling asleep. As the sky turned gray, we decided to skedaddle back to the wagons. We threw the three or four pounds of meat into a sack and hurried back.

As tired as I was, my mouth watered at the thought of the first meat in over a month. While we were sneaking back to camp, Jed turned and smashed me in the mouth with his fist. My knees buckled, and I fell. Wiping tears from my eyes, I jumped up and screamed, "What's got into you?"

Jed replied, "If either of you snitch about this ox, you'll get more every day until we reach Salt Lake." He continued, "I'm taking the meat. Ya gonna try and stop me?"

I shouldn't have expected anything different from that snake. He had bullied and pushed me around since the first day I saw him.

I readied myself. He saw me doubling up my fists and mockingly shook his head. "Stoner, you'll never learn."

He began rolling up his sleeves. While Jed was working out what form of beating he was going to give me, a horseman charged up and reigned in. Bishop Spiers had gotten up to round up strays. Being covered with mud and blood, he knew we had been up to something. "What you boys up this early for?"

Paul, nice and innocent like he was, simply was not prepared for sneaking around and stretching a truth or two, especially to a Bishop. He panicked and tossed the sack.

The Bishop peeked into the sack, and a knowing smile came to his face. "Well, it was right generous of you boys to spend the night getting this meat. I'm sure the whole train will enjoy sharing it."

From the look in Jed's eyes, I knew what was in store. That evening our share wasn't enough to put color in the soup pot.

The rest of the trip was one long battle. Jed took every opportunity to push me around. He knew I'd get mad and try to punch him. I got in a few good licks, but I always came out the worst of it. All my waking hours were spent dreaming of some way to get even. One Sunday, when the train was camped in South Pass, I got my chance.

Each Sunday the train camped. Church services were held in the wagon ring. The stock needed to be fed, so several of us would herd the animals to fresh grass. On that Sunday we didn't go far before we came to a good meadow. After sitting around most of the morning watching the herd, Paul and I figured we'd better start collecting strays.

Jed had ridden out, but we hadn't seen him all day. We figured stock might have wandered into thick willows near some beaver ponds. We started searching the banks.

After wandering a while, we found a large wasp's nest hanging from low branches. The willow was bent nearly to the ground. We kept our distance and continued along the creek.

A short distance further, I spotted the bay mare Jed had ridden. She stood tied near several tall cottonwoods. As we came closer, we saw that Jed's boots were in the saddle bags and his clothes were lying in a pile on the ground. We crept past the horse through the willows and came upon a large beaver pond. Lying asleep on the sand next to the pool was Jed, naked as a newborn babe.

I hushed Paul, and silently we sneaked away. When we got back to the horse I whispered, "Remember that wasp's nest?"

Paul turned white. "S . . . Sure."

"Let's play a trick."

Paul gulped. He knew what I planned and wanted none of it.

"Paul," I whispered, "you might as well help because Jed is going to blame both of us. If you don't help, I'll do it myself."

With that, I silently picked up Jed's pants and started back toward the wasp's nest. When we got in sight of the nest, I tied knots in the legs and charged. Shoving the nest inside, I squoze the waist around the branch that held the nest. Paul cut the branch with his jackknife.

We ran back to where the bay was tied. The wasps had stung me a couple of times, but I didn't care. As we neared the horse, Paul was in a panic. "Taw, let's forget about this and go back to the herd," he nervously squeaked.

I snarled, "Go hide, I'll do the rest."

I sneaked to Jed's shirt, untied the pant legs, and carefully set his pants on the ground in such a way that the waist and leg openings were underneath. The wasps couldn't escape until the pants were picked up. I felt mean so I picked up a stick and swatted the nest several times, enough to break it open. Lastly, I grabbed the picket rope on the bay and headed away from the creek. I swatted the bay, and she trotted up a small rise and stopped. She turned with ears pricked and looked at us. I knew she'd either join the herd or wander back to the wagon train.

We hid uphill from the pond. From where we lay, we could see both the pond and Jed's clothes. Jed must have seen his horse, because he suddenly stood up and looked in her direction. He started running through the shallow water until he disappeared behind the thick wall of bright green willows. We heard him crashing through the undergrowth. As he neared the clothes my heart raced. I had to hold Paul down to keep him from racing away. I put my hand over his mouth to keep him from hollering a warning. Appearing near his clothes, Jed swooped up his pants.

A dark cloud of bloodthirsty wasps swarmed out of the open waist. Jed froze! A horrid cloud descended upon him. He began swearing and swatting like a bear having a fit. He danced about the opening. In a swearing rage he ran back into the willows. After a moment he dove blindly into the beaver pond.

We couldn't tell where the wasps were, but Jed would swim under water for a while and come up for air. He'd be up just long enough to get a breath and dive under again. It was all I could do to keep from busting a gut with laughter. I looked over at Paul as he looked at me. With a sickly pale face he croaked, "Let's get out of here."

As we stood to leave, Jed surfaced, and, as luck would have it, he looked right at us before he disappeared under the muddy water. We ran around the hill hoping he hadn't seen us. Jed's horse had wandered back with the other animals. We bunched them and began moving back to the wagons. A few hours later we neared the wagons and hadn't seen Jed. Jason Spiers, one of the older boys who rode lookout, trotted up, pointing behind the herd. He remarked with a wink, "Sure got some strange looking Injuns in these parts."

We looked up and saw Jed striding through the sagebrush, naked as the day he was born. He was bright pink from sunburn, or maybe from wasp stings. We didn't want to get close enough to find out which. We knew trouble was a-coming, so we trotted out in front of the herd and hid ourselves inside one of the wagons. The entire camp rushed to see the strange sight. As Jed stomped into the ring of wagons, mothers shielded the tender eyes of their young girls. The men and boys whooped with laughter. I'm not sure how he ever explained to his pa how he lost his clothes when he wasn't supposed to be swimming because it was Sunday. It must have been a pretty good story.

Old Bishop Spiers figured that trouble was going to continue between me and Jed, so from that day until we reached the Salt Lake Valley, one of us stayed with the wagons while the other helped herd the stock. The rest of the wagon trip Jed never was never able to corner me when we were alone. He didn't forget, though, because a few days before we reached the Valley of the Great Salt Lake, he found me by the fire. "Taw," he said, "one day I'll get even for that stunt at the beaver pond." He turned and stomped away.

Knowing Jed, I figured he'd try.

One week later was a day I'll never forget. When we got up that morning, we were just ten miles from Salt Lake. This would be our last day on the trail. There was excitement everywhere. The animals even seemed to sense our journey was nearly ended.

Late that afternoon we crested a small rise and before us the valley opened up. To the northwest the Great Salt Lake shimmered, far bigger than I expected. Nestled against the foothills, the streets of Salt Lake were laid out in large squares.

But I must admit I was disappointed. Somehow I had expected a valley with thick grass reaching to a horse's belly.

Instead, I saw a valley filled with the same scrubby sagebrush that we had been seeing for the last hundred miles. A thin snake of willows wandered up the center of the valley, but over all it looked pretty dry and miserable.

I'll be danged if I could see what was so special about this place. But special or not, we'd just come a thousand miles to make this place home. I couldn't help wondering what my life here would be like.

Chapter Five

After we arrived in Salt Lake, Lars heard that John Sharp was hiring teamsters to haul rock from the quarry at Little Cottonwood Canyon to the Salt Lake Temple site. The quarry always needed teamsters, particularly if the teamster owned his own wagon and team.

The wagons used to haul granite blocks were the strangest I ever saw. The wheels were six feet tall so they could be loaded underneath, rather than on top. After stonecutters had cut and shaped a granite block, quarry workers would move it with log rollers to a flat place. After sliding straps underneath it, they would back a wagon over the stone. Using come-alongs and a block and tackle, they would hoist the stone off the ground and strap it on the underside of the wagon bed. This was easier than trying to load the two-ton stones on top of the beds. Fifteen to twenty wagons a day were loaded in this manner and began the journey to Salt Lake City.

The trip to Salt Lake from Granite took three or four days. Three days if you drove yourself and animals to exhaustion, and four days if you worked at a reasonable pace. Lars was not a reasonable man. He felt if you weren't bone weary at the end of the day, you had been loafing. That's the way he was, and he never changed.

Whenever I was doing chores and Lars was around, he would get after me to work faster and not dawdle. This got me going and made me want to slow down just to aggravate. Both of us wound up hollering back and forth. I looked forward to the times he was on his trips to the temple site.

Lars settled the family near the granite quarry in the little group of buildings that later became Granite City. Our home during that first summer was a couple of small tents that looked like Indian wickiups we'd seen on the trail. The tents were located near the pens holding the horses and oxen. Lars chose this site so one of us could keep an eye on the stock in case a mountain lion or Indian attempted to raid. He spent most of his time traveling to the temple site while the rest of us stayed home and put up with the stench of a large herd of oxen.

After a couple of months, I knew Lucy was on the verge of an eruption. Eight months earlier, she'd spent her weekends going to dances or taking long carriage rides with the sons of wealthy lawyers from Philadelphia. She'd been the guest at several parties where some of the most important people in Philadelphia were present. Like my ma, she turned heads wherever she went.

Back in Pennsylvania, Lucy had attended a fancy school and had been treated like a lady. In Utah Territory, she was spending twelve to fourteen hours a day cleaning and cooking for a bunch of brats that weren't even blood kin.

Utah Territory hadn't lived up to her expectations. When we moved into the wickiups, Lars explained it would be temporary until he built a house. He'd been so busy hauling rock to Salt Lake, he hadn't found the time to begin. Lucy gave Lars an ultimatum. "You better find yourself a wife," she said. "You better get that house built right away, or you will find four screaming kids riding that wagon with you, and I'll find someplace else to go."

Lars knew Lucy too well to doubt her word. That week, rather than make a second wagon trip to Salt Lake, Lars negotiated for a piece of ground and found a cabin we could stay in until he built a house. The cabin we moved into had two rooms and a dirt floor, but it was a vast improvement over the wickiups. Not being someone to dawdle, within three weeks Lars brought home a skinny little waif only a couple of years older than Lucy. She'd be our new ma. I looked at this skinny girl named Sarah, and then looked at the Swensen kids and shook my head—their mischievous brains were already figuring out ways to initiate her. She wouldn't last a week.

Chapter Six

Looking at Sarah, you'd have thought the first big wind would knock her over. At sixteen, Lucy had filled out and started looking like a lady. Sarah, at eighteen, still looked like a young girl. She wore her hair pulled back and tight to her head. Her two or three dresses were plain and looked alike.

To everyone's surprise, she turned out to be one tough stepmother. A week after she and Lars married, she had his ragamuffin kids under control. She laid out rules of how the house was going to run. Nobody dared to disagree—including Lars.

Sarah told Lars he could make only one trip a week until he finished her new house. She made Paul and me chop wood and run errands for one of the neighbors who paid us in boards. We made them into a wood floor for our cabin. Sarah didn't fool with Lucy, though. She knew it would take time for Lucy to accept her.

Sarah amazed Lucy. She accomplished twice the work around the place in half the time. Sarah even wound up with free time so she could think up all kinds of projects to keep Paul and me busy. She required all the kids to spend an hour a day studying books. She said this would do until September, when we'd go to school all day.

I told her what I thought. "I ain't going."

No sooner had I gotten the words out of my mouth than my skull was throbbing from a whack with a big metal spoon she carried in her knitting bag. I don't know how she got so handy with that spoon, but if I as much as made a face, my ears were ringing and a goose egg was growing out of my scalp. The same went for all the younger kids. Order came to the Swensen household, mostly out of the desire to not have our heads caved in.

Sarah's antics amused Lucy and yet puzzled her. Why would a skinny young girl like Sarah consent to become the wife of a man twenty years older? She could be pretty if she dressed up nice. Certainly, some young men her age would have an interest in courting her.

When my family first joined the Church, I hadn't heard anything about polygamy. At least the Elders who taught us about the Book of Mormon never spoke about it. I guess most of us were caught up with the Civil War and people didn't have much else on their minds. When we began traveling to Salt Lake, beginning with our first stop in Missouri, non-Mormons persecuted us mercilessly. They called us "polygs" and refused to sell us any goods from their stores. Feuding between the Saints and non-Mormons or gentiles followed us until we left Nebraska and headed across the plains. Persecution because of polygamy seemed the major reason the Saints kept their distance from gentiles.

While traveling across the plains, I never gave polygamy any thought—but Lucy did! Once she pulled me aside and asked, "What do the other boys say about polygamy while you're with the cattle?"

I gave her a strange look. "We could care less. We're always looking over our shoulder for Jed. We don't concern ourselves with such foolishness."

That didn't keep her from talking my ear off at the campfire. She had plenty of questions alright, and nobody to ask but me and Lars' brats. She felt embarrassed to speak to the older women, and few younger women spoke English. With Sarah in the house, Lucy had someone to answer the hundreds of questions crossing her mind.

Sarah had come across the plains as a young girl. She had heard stories how the Missouri mobs had robbed and killed the Saints, but couldn't remember it first hand. Shortly after Orson Pratt's announcement declaring polygamy as a celestial principle, Sarah's father had had a dream telling him to take a second wife. When Lucy heard this, she replied, "If my husband dreamt he should take a second wife, I'd have a dream. I'd see myself shooting any woman who tried to share his bed." Lucy wasn't much for hiding how she felt.

Sarah laughed, but she defended polygamy. She described how well her pa's three wives got along. He built each a separate house. Each of the older children had jobs and could be called on by any of the mothers to help. Sarah spent much of her time during her teenage years tending as many as eight runny-nosed kids at a time.

Sarah's father spent one week at each house. On Sundays the entire family got together. Each wife received equal time and attention, so none of the wives felt jealous. The three families got along so well the children grew up knowing little difference among the mothers. I found that hard to believe, since I had a hard enough time coping with one bossy older sister and Lars' brats. I don't think I could stand more.

Lucy asked, "How did your mother feel when your pa took a third wife?"

"It was my mother who arranged it," Sarah continued. "Father's other wife, Emily, suffered a lengthy illness after having a baby. Mother had her hands full and couldn't take care of Emily plus the ten children."

"Mother'd just met Phoebe Harris, who'd recently completed the journey across the plains. Phoebe's husband and young daughter died of cholera soon after leaving St. Joseph. Once Phoebe arrived in Salt Lake, she had no place to go. Mother invited her to help at our place. After several months,

Mother asked Phoebe if she'd like to become a sister-wife. Phoebe agreed, and Mother told Father that he was going to take another wife."

"You mean your mother arranged for a third wife," Lucy asked with surprise, "without asking your father first?"

"Mother liked Phoebe. She worked hard and had the sweetest spirit. Father was successful and provided for his family well. Mother knew sometime in the future he'd be asked by the brethren to take another wife. She wanted Father to marry someone she could get along with, not some stranger. It made sense at the time."

I had been listening to Sarah and Lucy talk, and I almost laughed. Knowing Lucy the way I did, I could imagine the kind of plural wife she'd pick. She wouldn't be a day under eighty. She'd have a toothless grin and a big hook nose.

This polygamy business didn't catch Lucy's fancy. The thought of a couple other wives eyeballing her husband when she wanted to do a little sparking didn't set well at all.

Within two months Lars finished our new house. It had two floors and was the nicest home in our part of the valley. It didn't take long for the Mormon farm boys to find Lucy. Soon, all kinds of fellas were calling. Lars insisted that somebody chaperon whenever one of the boys came to call—just like back in Pennsylvania. I became the unwanted guest.

With most of the boys, it was all the same. They'd sit for a spell, too embarrassed to speak. They'd start fidgeting and then blurt out something stupid about the weather. They'd get around to last night's sunset, then back to the weather. After throwing in a poorly-rehearsed compliment, they'd take one final pass at the weather. Flies would drop out of the air and die from sheer boredom. Lucy would sit and try to be gracious, but I could see the glaze in her eyes.

One boy in particular, Ollie Adamson, stood out. At least he made an impression with me. Ollie had the market cornered on ugly. His ears stuck out so far you'd have thought he was part mule. Half the beavers in the county were jealous of his fine set of buck teeth. He was the shyest boy I'd ever seen. When he knocked timidly on our door, Lucy answered. "Hello, Ollie," she said, visibly surprised. "What brings you here?"

He stood, frozen, unable to speak.

"Are you looking for Taw?"

He stared wide-eyed and shook his head.

"Do you need to see Lars?"

He shook his head faster.

Lucy, clearly growing impatient, tried to be pleasant. "Well then, Ollie, what do you want?"

Right then I'd have bet money that Ollie would turn and run. But somehow he croaked, "Lucy, I would be honored if you would accompany me on a . . . a . . . rarriage cide."

"A rarriage cide?" she questioned.

Ollie tried to speak but was too tongue-tied for anything to come out. His elephantine ears were glowing red. He finally gave up and pointed to the carriage he'd driven to our place.

Lucy smiled and looked thoughtful. I was sure she was thinking of some way to turn him down. She smiled, "Why, yes, I would like to go on a ride."

I was flabbergasted. Lucy could have her pick of any boy around, and she picked one that looked like he'd been kicked in the face with an iron-shod hoof. The carriage wouldn't hold the three of us, so Lars let Ollie borrow his buckboard.

Lucy sat on one side of the front bench, and Ollie was so far over on the other side that the slightest bump would have thrown him off. The first half hour we bumped along the road to Little Cottonwood Canyon. It seemed Ollie had used up his daily ration of words back at the house. He hadn't said a peep.

I laid in the back of the buckboard, sprawled on several sacks of grain. My only entertainment was to catch wood ants and flick them into Lucy's hair. So far she hadn't noticed.

Ollie, realizing he had better say something, tried to spit out the words. He worked his jaws, stuttered, stammered, and finally asked, "W . . . w . . . what do you think about the weather?"

All that effort wasted.

Lucy put up her hand. "Ollie, every boy that comes to see me talks about the weather. I'm not interested in that. Let's talk about something else. Why don't you tell me something about yourself."

He looked at her out of the corner of his eye and shrugged.

"What do you like to do?"

"Farm," came his meek reply.

Lucy rolled her eyes. "What do you farm?"

"Beets."

Lucy dropped her head into her hand and slowly shook her head. "Let's try again. I'll make it easier. What did you do earlier today?"

Ollie look sheepish and answered, "Castrated calves."

Whoa, that perked me right up. I'd run out of ants and was sprawled half asleep on the grain sacks. I shot up, stepped over the bench, and sat between Lucy and her courter. Then I spoke to Ollie, "Not being from the these parts, I've never cut a calf before. Tell me all about it, and don't leave any details out." I really had, but Ollie didn't know it.

Lucy started to object, but I reached behind her and put my hand over her mouth. My interest seemed to give Ollie newfound courage, and he started. "My Pa does the roping. After he snares one, he jumps off his gelding and throws it. Using a piggin string, he hog-ties the calf. Me and my brother foller behind."

"My brother notches the ears. That's so we can tell which baby belongs to which momma. While he's doing that, I go to work at the other end."

Lucy started squirming, trying to throw my hand away. Ollie didn't seem to notice. "I pull out my folding knife . . . I always use the folding knife . . . in fact, I got it right here in my pocket. See, that blood's from this morning."

"Keep going. Don't leave anything out," I egged him on. I was having a time keeping my hand over Lucy's mouth.

"I get the knife ready and make a quick grab with my left

hand. I wrap my middle finger and thumb around the . . ."

Slapping my hand away, she screeched, "E . . . NOUGH! Turn this wagon around. Taw, get in back!" She knocked me so that I fell over backward onto the sacks of grain. Ollie, realizing he'd stepped beyond the bounds of gentlemanly behavior, froze. Lucy jerked the reins away from him and slapped the horses.

Lucy galloped the team all the way home. I could almost see steam coming out her ears. She charged into the yard and jumped from the buckboard. She scurried around to Ollie's side. He'd already jumped to the ground. I expected her to tear into him, but she was calm. "I don't blame you for what happened," she said. "My brother tricked you into it."

She fired a glance that almost knocked me over. "I appreciate the ride today. I'm sure many girls would like your company. I don't think we're right for each other, though. Thank you again for a wonderful time." She reached over and kissed his cheek.

Turning to me, she glared and stormed into the house. Ollie had just got kissed by the prettiest girl around. His head was in the clouds. He took his cue and jumped into his carriage and trotted away. I jumped off the buckboard and began walking the team to the stalls. I could hear Lucy's shouting and carrying on all the way out to the barn. Occasionally I'd hear the crash of something she'd thrown. Lars' booming voice started hollering back. Soon the door slammed, and he came charging out to begin tearing into me.

We hollered back and forth a might. I didn't get nervous until I saw Sarah high-stepping toward the barn with her metal spoon. I jumped astride one of the team and trotted out of the yard. I didn't want anything to do with that spoon. I kept myself scarce for a few hours.

When I returned, Sarah laid out the law. "The next time you go on a carriage ride, I'll be waiting in the yard. If you haven't been a perfect gentleman, your head will be ringing for a week. You understand?"

I knew better than to cross her.

So, I spent every Sunday as an unwanted guest. All I could do was suffer in silence. After a few months, it seemed the only way to end it was if Lucy got hitched. I made it my job to do everything possible to get her to take the step. I tried to point out all her suitors' good traits. With most of them, it took some real looking to find anything worth talking about.

When Lucy went to Salt Lake to help Sarah's sick sister, I spread word that Lucy had run off to get hitched. That slowed the farm boys for a spell, but one of Lars' brats told Sarah and I got whacked.

I was plumb desperate. I had to find someone to take my place. I needed a surefire plan, one that was guaranteed to work. Of course, any fair plan wouldn't do that, so I'd have to cheat. I had to find someone so naive and trusting that he wouldn't expect a mean and rotten trick. The natural choice was Paul.

Several months before, Paul had cleared brush for the Sheffields, who farmed down the road. They paid him with several young roosters. One of them turned into the fightenest rooster I'd ever seen. Paul spent hours training that bird. I'd seen it make full-grown dogs back down.

Paul had gone to all the nearby farms to fight his bird. It was never a contest. Paul's bird always won. He named him Paiute Pete, and all the sporting folk in these parts soon knew the name.

I'd tried all kinds of ways to get Paul to take my place on the carriage rides. I asked, begged, threatened, and tried to bribe him. But I couldn't get him to see it my way. He could tell by how much I hated it that it must be worse than getting kissed by a girl.

I tried everything. The only thing left was to make a bet I couldn't lose. Paul was so cocked sure he had the best rooster in these parts he'd take any bet, even if losing meant taking my place on the carriage rides. All I had to do was find a rooster that could beat Paiute Pete.

I couldn't do that, but I had a plan.

I bought a rooster from a family in Granite. After bragging

him up, I had Paul slobbering all over himself to have the two birds fight. "Put your money where your mouth is," he told me. "Let 'em fight."

I refused. "Paul, you must think I'm crazy. You got to make it worth my while. This here bird of mine has rare fighting ability."

I couldn't just pipe up and mention the carriage rides. Even Paul could smell a trick if I made it too obvious. I had to make the bet for the carriage rides seem like his idea. We haggled back and forth. After a couple of days, we finally worked out a deal. If Paiute Pete lost, Paul had to go on the carriage rides for six months. If his rooster won, I had to milk the cows for the same time. It was a one-sided bet. Both of us would rather milk. But Paul was so cocked sure he'd win he didn't care.

It was almost too easy. Paul wanted to fight the birds the moment we shook hands. "I'm sorry," I answered. "My bird has a special disposition. He fights best at sun-up."

Paul groused and moaned, but agreed to wait.

Late that night after everyone was asleep, I snuck over to the barn. Lighting my way with a candle, I crept to the pen where Paul kept his bird and threw a sack over Paiute Pete. A few weeks earlier I'd found a chaw of tobacco in the road. It was covered with dirt, but I figured it might come in handy.

Back in Pennsylvania I heard men talk about chewing tobacco, and they always said that if you swallowed the juice you'd get a powerful stomachache. If chewing tobacco could make a man sick, it ought to do the same to a fighting rooster. I wrestled with Paiute Pete and finally used my thumb to pry open his beak. I began stuffing small pieces of brown tobacco down the bird's gizzard.

I stuffed Ol' Pete as full as I dared and then let him go. He spurred me and looked as mean as ever. The more he strutted, the more it looked like the bet wouldn't turn out the way I'd planned. I didn't know what else to do, so I turned in and hoped for the best.

The cock's crowing stirred me awake. I had a sick feeling.

Paul was already pulling on his pants. He couldn't wait to see Paiute Pete knock the stuffing out of my bird. He gathered the whole family to go watch the big fight. Paul was strutting just like his rooster. He kept saying how good it would be to be buried in his warm quilts while I was out milking.

We all walked to the bird pens, and Paul was so excited he had trouble opening the latch. The pen was dark and Paul had to reach way back inside to catch Ol' Pete. When Paul hauled out his bird, it was clear that something was wrong. If it's possible for a chicken to look green, that's the way Pete looked. Paul usually had his hands full trying to keep from being pecked and spurred, but now that rooster was as docile as a kitten. I had to turn my head to keep Paul from seeing me smiling.

Paul set him down. Usually Pete fluffed up his hackle feathers and high-stepped. Instead, he just stood and wavered on his feet.

A panicked look spread across Paul's face, and he snatched up Pete. "What's the matter, fella? You sick?"

In the meantime, I had pulled my rooster from his pen and had him raring to go. "Come on Paul, put 'em down. Let 'em go at it."

"Nothing doing. Something's wrong with Pete. I never seen him like this. Must have been something he ate."

If only he knew.

"Hold on here. We had a bet. You're just afraid of this fine rooster of mine." I pretended to be angry.

"It ain't so," Paul hollered back. "My bird's sick. He can't fight now. He'll be better tomorrow."

I answered, "My bird's got a delicate disposition. He's all raring to go. I can't disappoint him. It may ruin him. We'll fight now."

We went back and forth like this for twenty minutes. All the brothers and sisters who had come out to see the fight got bored and wandered back to the house.

I settled on calling off the fight, as long as Paul kept his side of the bet. Paul was relieved that Paiute Pete wasn't going to have to fight, and I did the best acting job of my life trying to look disappointed that the fight had been called off.

Within a few days Paiute Pete was back to his nasty old self, but by that time my rooster had become a tasty dutch oven dinner. Paul never suspected his stepbrother could stoop low enough to feed his chicken chewing tobacco. Over the next several months, whenever Paul came back from one of the carriage rides, I had a good chuckle. I never told him what took the fight out of Ol' Paiute Pete.

I continued my war of wills with Lars. Maybe I still blamed him for losing Ma. But, whatever Lars wanted me to do, that was what I least wanted to do. Things were relatively quiet when Lars was on one of his trips, but on the days he was at home, the hollering started at sunup and lasted until dark.

Most of the hollering occurred because I wouldn't go to church. I don't really know why I wouldn't go, but the harder Lars tried to force me to, the more I fought against it. Usually, the whole family was late by the time he got me in the wagon. As soon as we arrived at church, I'd jump off and run home.

I guess going to church brought back the memories of Ma dying. Every time I'd ride up to the ward house, all I could think about was the wagon sliding into the river. I'd been told in Sunday meetings if you tried to live right and prayed for blessings, you'd be protected. The morning before Ma died, we prayed for safety, and look what happened to her.

Ma was the best women I'd ever known. If anybody had troubles, she was there to help. A day didn't pass that she didn't read out of the Bible or Book of Mormon. Yet, she still drowned. I figured that if bad things were still going to happen, why pray at all?

After Lars came home from church, he'd give me a whuppin. I didn't care. The same thing would happen the next week. Finally, he decided he was beating his head against a wall, and he stopped trying. When he stopped trying to force me to go to church, the hollering stopped. But it was an uneasy truce.

It was best that I stayed away from him when he was home.

I have to admit that although Lars and I constantly battled about church, he never treated me different from his kin. Sure, he owned a quick temper and yelled all the time, but he treated me like one of his own and never gave up. He even went out of his way to see me when he came home from his trips to Salt Lake. At least for a little while.

At times you look at your life and regret the way you did things. Lars had his faults—he was impatient and had a hot temper—but he tried to be a pa to me. I never gave him a chance.

Chapter Seven

In 1869, the railroad reached Utah Territory—the year I turned sixteen. The Swensen house had become almost peaceful. Lars and I had worked out a truce. We hadn't actually sat down and talked it through, but he knew I wasn't going to church, and I did my work around the farm and didn't cause trouble.

Lars still hauled granite from the mouth of the canyon, and so was gone most of the week. I helped out at the farm and had started taking jobs from neighbors hauling goods on a wagon Lars helped me build.

Though we argued about most things, Lars' ideas about working made sense. He felt a man had to work for himself in order to get anywhere. He encouraged me to build and haul with my own wagon and teams, rather than hire on and use someone else's. That way, if things didn't work out, I could always put my things together and find other work. It made sense. I was paid top wages for having my own team and wagon, and I never had trouble finding work.

In the spring of the year I turned seventeen, Lars took the whole family to a barn raising for one of the members of our ward. Orson Smith had recently moved his family to a farm not far from where we lived. I normally didn't go to these kind of things, but Orson Smith had a daughter, Julina, who, as far as I was concerned, was the prettiest girl in these parts. Though Julina was only sixteen and five years younger than Lucy, they had become good friends. There weren't many girls in these parts, and Lucy had gotten to know Julina from church meetings.

Lucy had spoken to me about Julina often and told me Julina was pretty enough for me to go to church for. I wasn't going to fall for that trick. I'd seen Julina about town, but since I never went to church I'd never had a chance to talk to her. I hoped I'd get that chance at the barn raising.

I wasn't the only one who'd fallen for Julina. She turned almost as many heads as Lucy did. She had long, reddish-brown hair that hung to the middle of her back. She was about average height, with green eyes that sparkled when she laughed. From what Lucy told me, she was always surrounded by a pack of boys at church meetings. The barn raising was going to be my big chance to make a good impression.

The barn site was located near a large corral where a milk cow had given birth to twin calves the night before. Twin calves were rare, so everybody walked over to take a look. I'd been working most of the morning when I noticed that Julina was leading a group of young children to get a look. Putting a blade of grass in my teeth, I wandered over next to the corral fence and leaned up against it. I figured I'd get a chance to talk to her.

Being March, the corral was a mucky mess of manure-tinted pools. As the children leaned over the fence, the cow became increasingly upset. The calves were in two different corners, so she nervously paced between them. One of the kids threw a rock at a calf. The calf bawled. With that the cow began to throw muck with her front hooves in preparation for a charge. The kids scattered, and Julina followed them.

As she passed, I reached out, grabbed her hand and said, "Julina, there's nothing to worry about. This fence is made of solid cedar posts. That cow will stop before she comes to the fence."

Julina pulled her hand away and said, "I'm not about to stay here if that cow is going to charge." She scurried away.

I hoped that she would see the foolishness of being afraid of a cow that couldn't possibly break through such a strong corral.

I had turned my back to the corral while talking to Julina, and the cow charged directly at me. As I turned, I saw the cow coming. I felt Julina would be impressed by my lack of concern. I was a man now, and a man is not afraid of things that can't harm him.

As the cow loomed, Julina screeched, "Are you crazy? She is coming right at you. Get away!"

I just chuckled and said, "Wait, she'll stop."

Sure enough, six feet before she reached the fence, the cow locked up both front legs and slid to a stop. What I hadn't planned on was the huge wave of manure-laden mud and cow slobber that arched toward me. Determined to show my lack of fear, I had started laughing. My mouth was still open when the wave hit me in the face, knocking me to the ground.

With manure in my mouth, nose, eyes, and ears, I rose up, gasping and swearing, to the great entertainment of the children and Julina. The uproarious laughter brought everyone else to the corral. There I was, kneeling on the ground, trying not to gag.

The onlookers roared as I crawled to the pump. Somebody pumped while I laid under the freezing stream, trying to wash off.

I'd come to the barn raising hoping to make a good impression, but I wound up looking like the town fool. I got cleaned off. Lars had spare clothes, so I changed behind the barn. The legs were short and the belly too big, but I wasn't in a position to complain. I spent the rest of the day watching kids strut up to the corral and say, "There's nothing to worry about." Then they'd pretend to get knocked flat. It was the longest afternoon of my life.

Late in the afternoon, I wound up working with Paul behind the barn. Every time he looked at me, he broke out laughing. I threatened to skin him alive. He tried to stop, but every few minutes he'd chuckle and shake his head.

As we were handing boards up to the boys working in the loft, a wagon pulled into the yard. I didn't pay any mind. All I could think about was what Julina must be thinking. I decided it would be easier to forget her . . . but she was just too pretty. I figured I'd have to say something to her so she wouldn't forever think of me as such a fool.

While Paul and I were lifting boards, I tried to figure some way to begin a conversation. I couldn't come up with any good ideas, just a bunch of bad ones. So, I decided to walk up to her when she was alone and start talking.

I got my chance when I saw she had wandered over to the hillside on the far side of the spring to pick wildflowers. I told Paul, "I'll be right back."

I hurried out of the barn, leaving Paul holding a board that was too big for him to pass to the boys in the loft. "Get back here!" he hollered. But I waved him off and hustled toward Julina.

A trail led down the hill to the spring. A thick growth of scrub oak grew along the path, which wound through the oaks and up the hill.

As I walked through the oaks, I stumbled upon several others about my age. They had snuck away from the barn raising and were sharing a couple of bottles of Valley Tan. I had no idea where they'd gotten the whiskey, but by the way they acted when I appeared, they knew they weren't supposed to have it. I chuckled and was about to walk on when I took a second look. The one standing in the middle had a face I could never forget . . . it was Jed Mathews!

The same Jed Mathews who'd made my trip across the plains so miserable years before. It had been years since I'd seen him. His family had been living in St. George. He looked the same—but different. He'd taken on the build of a man now. His looks would blind most girls to the mean streak that lay underneath. I glanced at the other two with Jed and remembered them as his older brothers. They were huskier than Jed and several inches taller.

I had changed a might. I still had dark brown eyes and light brown hair, but I wasn't the skinny eleven-year-old that was six inches shorter than Jed. I was near his height. My arms were strong and my shoulders wide. I could handle myself in a scrape.

Jed and his brothers didn't say anything, but I saw recognition spread across his face and a wicked glint came to his eyes. He said, "Boys, remember that skinny Stoner kid who stole my clothes in South Pass?" The brothers continued sucking on the bottle, but Jed swaggered over to me and said, "I never got a chance to pay you back for those clothes of mine you stole."

With that he gave me a shove in the shoulder.

It caught me by surprise. All the dislike and anger I'd felt for him years before rushed back. I remembered the times he'd thrown me to the ground and ground my face in the dirt, the bloody noses, and the stolen food. He'd been able to get away with it because he was bigger and older. The years had taken that advantage away, and Jed would have his hands full if he picked a fight with me now.

But maybe I had underestimated Jed. He never picked a fight he couldn't win. After he pushed me, he slowly circled, and as he did I turned to face him. When his brothers were to my back, he stopped. Then he sneered, "Stoner, you've grown a might since I last saw you. Maybe you even think you can whup me. But you never will." He let out a taunting laugh and continued, "You just ain't smart enough, and you'll never be man enough."

I almost threw a punch, but I suddenly thought about Julina. After everything that had happened today, if I was to beat up one of her family's guests, surely she'd never speak to me. As much as I hated doing it, I raised my two hands and said, "Jed, I got no quarrel with you. Our problems were over years ago. I just want to walk up that hill and talk to that girl up there."

Jed gave me a shocked look. He looked beyond me, and

then with a mean grin said, "What makes you think you have the right to speak to my girlfriend? Since her sister married my brother Nate, I've been seeing her quite regular."

He stepped to me so that his face was inches from mine and shouted, "Besides, Stoner, she won't have anything to do with someone of your kind."

While Jed had been speaking, his brothers had moved up behind me, and Jed suddenly shoved me toward them. I staggered backwards, and his two brothers grabbed me, pinning my arms. He stepped to me and said, "I'm going to teach you to never bother my gal again."

With that he threw a left that grazed my cheek as I ducked. I tried to twist out of the way, but his brothers held me tight. He threw another punch that I slipped, but his right hit me in the ribs, and his left knocked the air out of me when it connected with my stomach.

The punch doubled me over. Jed's brothers straightened me up, and Jed measured me and a punch connected to my mouth. I felt my head snap to the side. My blood splattered over the shirt of one of his brothers. Another punch hit me in the cheek, and it felt like my face exploded.

Jed continued throwing his fists. He threw so many I couldn't count. I tried to break loose, but his brothers were too strong. Dropping to my knees, I felt myself slipping into unconsciousness. A boot pushed me onto my side into the shallow water.

I laid in the spring with the side of my face in the water. With my one open eye I could see a small trickle of blood spread across the surface. I pulled myself up. Jed and his brothers were gone. I must have been out, because I hadn't remembered them leaving.

I felt my face. It was a swollen and bloody mess. My ribs hurt, and I was soaking wet from lying in the spring. I felt like a calf that had been roped, thrown, and branded. I stood and decided I could walk. The last place I wanted to go was back to the barn raising. I didn't want everybody laughing at me again.

I hurried along the spring to the road and back to our place. I tried the best I could to doctor my wounds. It seemed hopeless. My right eye was swollen shut, and my teeth were loose. The ribs on my left side felt broke. It hurt to breathe. It hurt to swallow, and it hurt thinking about how Jed had got the best of me. What hurt most of all was Jed courting Julina. The thought made me want her all the more. Somehow I'd find a way to talk to her.

I stayed out of sight for a few days, but not because I was afraid of Jed. I ached for a chance to meet him without his brothers. But I didn't want to have to tell anybody what happened.

By the time I was up and around, my bruises had mostly healed. A few noticed my black eye, but I growled and acted mean when asked about it. The cow incident was bad enough. Every time I turned around, some kids were acting it out. Had I told people about the fight, I would have had to watch another round of play acting.

Jed and his family had been visiting from their home in St. George. Lucy told me Julina's older sister had married one of Jed's older brothers. Julina frequently traveled to St. George to visit her, and Jed courted Julina whenever she visited.

Later that week I drove my wagon to Sandy City to pick up some parts from the dry goods store. While I was waiting at the counter, a female voice came from behind me and said, "If it isn't Taw Stoner, the boy who isn't afraid of cows."

I wheeled, angered by the comment, when I caught the sparkling green eyes of Julina Smith. She looked lovely, wearing a blue dress with her hair softly falling on her shoulders. I stood as if struck dumb, not saying anything. She broke the silence, saying "Taw, anyone who could stand up to a charging cow couldn't be afraid of me."

I was surprised; I didn't know that she knew my name. I felt my ears turning red and figured I'd better say something or I'd look like an even bigger fool. I stammered, "Julina, you surprised me. Guess I didn't expect to see you."

She looked at me coyly and asked, "What are you in town for?"

"Picking up supplies." I gulped. My mouth was dry.

Swirling her finger in some flour dust on the counter, she asked, "Are you going home after this?"

"Sure," I said, looking at her too long.

"How handy," she said with a twinkle. "Driving into town today, one of the wheels on my carriage broke. The blacksmith told me it would take most of the day to repair." Looking into my eyes, she put her hand on my arm and said, "If you don't mind, maybe I could ride back with you. I'll send one of my brothers back to pick up the carriage tomorrow."

Boy, did she know how to flirt! My heart soared. I tried not to be too excited, but I was. "Sure, you can ride with me," my voice cracked.

Julina smiled an impish smile.

A short while later I helped her onto the seat of my wagon and, clucking at my horses, started back to Emmaville. I couldn't believe it. I'd been hoping for a chance to talk with Julina, yet now that we were alone I felt tongue-tied and couldn't think of anything clever to say.

I got nervous. My palms got wet. I had to say something. I babbled something about how pretty the mountains were and the weather. How stupid! I looked at her and could tell she'd heard it all before.

I figured I should try and explain about the incident at the corral. I started, "Julina, I've been bothered about how I must have looked the other day at your place."

She chuckled, "You mean when the wave of corral mud hit you in the face?"

"No . . . I don't mean that. I mean . . . ."

She jumped in, "When you were lying on the ground gagging up the manure."

"No." This was not going well at all. "Not then . . . ."

"You mean when you were changing behind the barn?"

"No . . ." I began, and then it hit me. "YOU SAW ME

CHANGING?"

She answered with an air of indifference, "While you were taking off your wet clothes. All of us girls had gone to the house to get the lunch. When we came outside, there you were."

"You mean you came outside before I'd started?"

"No."

"Then you walked outside after I'd put on Lars' clothes."

"Nope."

Flabbergasted I said, "You mean you saw me . . . naked!"

She tried to hold back a laugh as she answered, "Don't worry. We all have brothers." She added thoughtfully, "Except the Hulet girls, but they didn't stare too long."

In a weak voice I asked, "How many of you were there?"

"Only seven. Maybe ten," she laughed.

I almost fell off the wagon. She saw the look on my face and laughed all the harder. When she'd caught her breath she said, "I got a good laugh the other day. You were acting like a know-it-all and deserved what happened. But I still thought you were good looking. Even in Lars' clothes."

Then she added, "By the time we girls came out of the house, you'd put on Lars' pants. I thought you needed a little teasing."

I should have been mad, but I melted with one look into her green eyes. We bumped along the dusty road, and I hardly noticed the time passing. We talked and laughed. Before I knew it, we came to Willow Creek.

I stopped to let the horses water, but mostly to spend a little more time with Julina. The water of the small creek looked so clean and cold on such a hot day. Julina sat up and asked, "Don't you love the feeling of walking in the creek mud and feeling it squish up between your toes?"

Before I could answer, she had taken off her shoes and was ankle-deep in the mud on the sand bar. I sat on the wagon and watched her as she wiggled her toes in the brown mud. She looked up at me and said, "What's the matter with you?" and kicked mud and water at me. A glob of mud hit me in the forehead.

I jumped down from the wagon, and pulling off my boots, began chasing her and kicking water on her. She laughed and tried to keep out of the reach of my spray. We ran around until we came to a pool filled with tadpoles. Julina said, "Taw, ever since I was a little girl I've loved to catch tadpoles."

Together, we chased around the pool, grabbing at the slimy tadpoles. We'd grab one, only to have it slither away. After a while, we found ourselves sitting on the bank, hanging our feet in the cool water. Julina's hair was out of place, and little splatters of mud dotted her nose. With the hem of her dress she wiped the mud from my face, and I tried to do the same for her.

Her eyes sparkled as we talked, and I found myself wanting to hold her and kiss her. I guess she could tell as much by the look in my eyes, because she suddenly stood up. She held out her hand, and as I took it and stood, she took a step forward and stood close to me. I was certain she wanted a kiss. She was so lovely! Looking into her eyes, I leaned down to kiss her.

To my shock, she gave me a shove. I staggered backward, falling into the water. Sitting up, I looked to see her laughing as she raced back to the wagon. I stood up and did the best I could to act mad, but gave up by the time I reached the wagon.

As I climbed on the wagon and sat next to her, she said, "You don't think I'd kiss a boy I hardly knew, do you?"

I replied sheepishly, "I'd hoped so."

"Well, now you know."

We arrived all too soon at the Smith home. After helping Julina from the wagon, I asked, "May I call on you sometime?"

She replied, "I'd like that." She reached up on her tiptoes and gave me a quick kiss on the lips. Then she scampered into the house.

I'll never figure women out.

Over the rest of the summer I called on Julina every couple of weeks. Every time I saw her I fell in love all over again. She was always happy and fun to be with. She wasn't shy like some of the girls I'd known. She wasn't afraid to speak her mind. If I disagreed with her on something, I had to be certain of my facts. She read more than anybody I'd met.

The things she told me made me wish I'd paid more attention in school. At times I felt foolish, having never heard of the things and places she talked about.

I wasn't the only fellow trying to impress Julina. At times, I'd get discouraged because I'd drop by her house and find some other boy was already there. Yet, Lucy would encourage me to keep seeing her. The rest of that summer I never got another chance to kiss her.

Chapter Eight

The coming of the railroad changed everyone's life. Years before, prospectors had found low-grade silver ore in most of the nearby canyons. But the ore was of too poor quality to make mining pay. With the coming of the railroad, that all changed. Ore could be hauled to San Francisco, and money could be made.

Soon, prospectors were staking claims all over the hillsides of the nearby canyons. Many of the men living nearby and from Sandy City filed claims at the head of Little Cottonwood Canyon. Most of the early prospectors were farmers or shop owners. They typically mined for a few days and returned to their homes. They'd spend a week or more catching up on the chores, then return for a few more days of mining. Many found ore, but the ore wasn't rich enough to cause any excitement.

Few had enough money to properly develop their claims, so mining continued as small one-man operations. Very little ore made its way down the canyon.

In the early spring of 1871, the year I turned eighteen, a man named Woodhull made a discovery on the north side of Little Cottonwood Canyon, about a mile east of Central City, that sent a tremor through the territory—a vein of silver ore richer than any seen before. The mine was named Emma, and she made headlines all the way to the East Coast.

It's been said that nothing travels like bad news, but that ain't so. Nothing travels like the news of a rich vein. Within weeks, a stream of men began arriving by train, making their way to the head of Little Cottonwood Canyon. Central City, a small group of mining shacks at the top of the canyon, was soon swallowed up by the new town of Alta.

In the midst of all this excitement, Brigham Young warned the men in Salt Lake to stay away from mining. "It's an immoral activity," he preached. "Any decent person should not become involved."

I've noticed that dreams of riches can dull even a pious man's hearing. Few men gave up their claims. Lars talked me out of selling my teams and wagon and staking a claim. "For every miner who strikes it rich, a hundred starve," he said. "I've seen it before. In a mining boom, the people who make the most money are those who sell goods or haul for the miners. Haul ore for a few months. You can always prospect later on."

I never agreed with Lars on many points, but I respected his business sense. I figured I'd give what he said a try. I had to admit that thoughts of riches kept me occupied, and that was the main reason I didn't call on Julina more. The wagon trips I made to Salt Lake hauling ore were long. The odd times in a month I spent a night at Lars' place I'd try to see Julina, but that wasn't often.

After picking up a load, I hauled it to the rail head in Salt Lake. A round trip took four or five days. As soon as I arrived in Alta, another load of ore always waited.

Each time I'd drop in on Julina, I'd get all jumpy on the inside. I'd gaze into her eyes, hold her soft hand, and think about marrying her. But it was several weeks before I'd see her again. After a few days on the trail, I'd figure I was a fool. Several other boys were spending more time with her. She'd fall for one of them first. I'd never have a chance. Besides, she'd want to marry somebody who'd take her to church. Julina was a very pretty girl, and I thought about her plenty. But I'd made my mind up about church, and I wasn't going to change for anybody.

Within a few weeks after I started hauling, I had all the work I could handle. Since I hauled big loads and didn't dawdle, I was paid top wages. I was making more money than I'd even dreamed possible one year before. The way things were going, within a couple of years I'd have enough saved to buy my own farm. I didn't know many doing as well.

The silver mines in Alta were making it all possible for me. Month after month my poke was growing. By the time the summer of 1871 rolled around, life couldn't have looked better.

But good things never last, and that was the case in Alta. That summer it was as if a mangy, shaggy old wolf stole into town and shook off all its vermin and lice. A new wave of outsiders trekked up the steep canyon, seeking their fortunes.

The first wave to move into Alta had been miners looking to find and work their own claims. They were rough men who liked liquor and women, but they worked hard and only wanted an opportunity to strike it rich. This next bunch was nothing more than murderers and thieves—too lazy to do their own work, only hoping to steal what earlier prospectors had already dug from the ground.

The newcomers were smart. They easily gained control of the mining districts and rewrote the rules for keeping a claim active. If a miner fell behind on his taxes or did not work his claim often enough, another miner could claim ownership by paying the taxes or by challenging that the mine had not been worked.

Most of the early mines were worked by one or two men. It usually took a week or two of work to dig out enough ore to make a trip to Salt Lake worthwhile, so the ore would pile up in front of their mines until there was enough to fill a wagon. Most of the claims were not producing enough high-grade ore for a man to work full time and feed his family. Instead, the miners spent most of their week working on their farms down in the valley and a few days working their claims in Alta.

Few kept their taxes current or kept records of how often they worked. More than once, a Mormon miner visited his family and then returned to the mine, only to find someone else working his claim. The claimjumpers would state that the claim had been abandoned or not worked as required by the rules of the mining district. Frequently, the claim-jumpers would even have paid the back taxes to justify their position.

Mormon miners felt that they were being cheated, but there wasn't much they could do because they found themselves outmanned and outgunned. Nevertheless, some tried to fight for their claims. Most claim disputes were settled at the Grand Hotel or Brandy's Restaurant and Saloon. The claimjumpers usually won. Many unlucky claimholders made their last trip down the canyon in a pine box or to the cemetery in Collins Gulch. The sight was always the same: A grieving widow, with several small children clinging to her skirt.

This was the way of life at Alta during the rest of 1871 and into 1872. By the time the summer of 1872 rolled around, you couldn't expect to hold onto a claim unless you were handy with a Colt.

After seeing friends killed, many of the original miners tried to sell out. The claimjumpers just laughed. They had no intention of paying for a claim they could simply move in on and take over. Most of the original miners gave up and abandoned their claims. The claimjumpers moved onto these and entertained themselves by shooting each other.

The grave diggers worked overtime throughout 1871. With all the lead flying, finding a sheriff for Alta was no small task. The town finally found a man, but he spent his time proving the most recent shootings had been acts of self-defense. That way, he didn't have to risk his neck trying to catch killers.

The Mormons living in Alta finally started listening to Brigham Young. They either moved to Tanner, a few miles down the canyon, or to the granite quarry at the mouth of the canyon.

After seeing the changes in Alta between the spring of 1871

and 1872, my enthusiasm for the work there wavered. Sure, I was making money faster than rabbits make bunnies, but what good was money if I was dead? It seemed every time I came back for another load, another man I knew had been shot. Men had died for a careless word or arguing over the cost of a drink. At any given moment, bumping into the wrong man in a saloon could leave you lying in a pine box, pushing up daisies. I didn't take to pine boxes.

Each time I rode out of town, I breathed a sigh of relief. As I bumped along the trail, I spent plenty of time trying to talk myself into quitting while I was still breathing. All the way to the rail depot, I argued with myself. I had plenty of reasons to not go back. But the lure of just one more trip and one more payday was more than I could ignore. Greed kept me hauling through my nineteenth birthday and into the fall of 1872.

Chapter Nine

It was just after the leaves turned that Lucy sprang the news. She was going to get hitched. While teaching school in Salt Lake, she'd met the man of her dreams. He was handsome and important. I didn't know much about him, but Lucy said she was in love and he would make her happy. So I was glad for her.

I knew hearts were breaking all over the territory. Some of those farm boys had been calling on her for five years. When she moved to Salt Lake, many of our local boys would ride all the way from Emmaville to see her. But she wanted somebody who had more than horses, cows, and planting on his mind.

I didn't think Lucy would find anybody like that in this territory. I always told her she shouldn't be so picky. Most of the other girls her age were already married and had babies. That didn't worry her, though I think she would have become an old maid rather than marry somebody she didn't love. She had found somebody, and I could tell when I heard her talk that she loved him and wanted to be with him forever.

The week after Lucy was married, she came to Lars' place to put together some of her things. I was between hauling jobs and offered to take her belongings to Salt Lake. I'd loaded the wagon first thing and helped with the chores. When I walked back, I was surprised to see Julina with Lucy, waiting in the wagon. Julina had gone to St. George since her sister had recently had a baby. She'd been gone for several months, and I wasn't aware she'd returned. Lucy had received letters from Julina, and told me Jed had been seeing Julina while she stayed in St. George. The thought of Jed Mathews calling on her made my blood boil, but I didn't say anything.

I climbed aboard and found the three of us cozy on the seat. Julina wrinkled her nose at me and said, "I hope you don't mind me coming with you."

My heart raced as I said, "You can ride with me anytime."

Julina was seated in the middle, and I found myself sitting closer to her than I ever had before. My heart fluttered like the wings of a bee. As we rolled out of the yard, a wheel dropped into a large hole, and Julina grabbed hold of my arm to steady herself. Her grip lingered, and when I looked at her, she was gazing into my eyes.

I could tell this was going to be an enjoyable trip. Lucy said something about why Julina had come along, but I didn't hear her. My thoughts were all on those green eyes.

I drove slowly. I wanted this trip to last forever. We journeyed up the dusty road as the girls caught me up on all the gossip around town.

Along the road, rainbow-bellied lizards scampered away from the plodding horses. A pair of redtail hawks lazily circled above us, hoping we'd scare up some varmints. The scrub jays scolded us endlessly from the brush lining the trail. But I paid none of them any heed. My eyes and ears were all on Julina.

She told me about her life in St. George, that it was mostly hot and boring. Occasionally, an old Piede would get drunk and cause some kind of trouble. All told, she was glad to be back, and I didn't mind her saying that a bit. But still, I couldn't get the thought of Jed calling on her out of my head. I wisely held my tongue.

When Julina talked she was quick to laugh, and when she did her eyes twinkled and two little dimples came to her cheeks. Her laugh wasn't loud or harsh, but smooth and pleasant. I enjoyed watching her face when she spoke. One moment she would look shocked, and then her face would light up with a smile. She'd pout and then break into her wonderful laugh. She was so filled with a love of life that just talking to her was a joy.

The time passed so quickly that I hardly noticed. I tried to be a gentleman and include Lucy in our conversation, but by the impatient looks Lucy was giving me, I must not have been doing a very good job. Ah, heck; I could talk to my sister anytime.

We stopped at Cottonwood Creek and watered the horses. A breeze picked up and blew away the mid-morning heat. The horses enjoyed the coolness. They picked up their gait and flared their nostrils. As we continued along, gusts set the treetops to waving. Dark, billowy clouds charged over the western hills. In the distance thunder rumbled. I pulled the slicker from under my seat, and I offered it to Lucy and Julina.

The first drops of rain raised puffs of dust as they hit the ground. The puffs were scattered at first, but soon the drops came faster. The breeze and the smell of rain excited the horses. They tossed their heads and pulled at the reins. Their pace quickened, and I had to hold them back from breaking into a trot.

The rain became a downpour, and I pulled my hat down and raised my collar. Lucy and Julina were holding the slicker over their heads like a tent. Julina peeked at me from under the slicker and puckered her lips. I thought about tipping the brim of my hat and dripping water down her back. I decided that would be too mean. Then Julina reached out with her hand and whipped some dirt across my cheek.

All bets were off. I pulled back the slicker and, leaning back, tipped my hat so that a stream of water trickled down the back of Julina's neck.

She let out a high-pitched squeal, and the horses bolted. The sudden movement threw me off balance, and it was all I could do to keep from toppling onto Lucy's possessions. I found myself trying to slow the charging horses while lying on my back across the wagon seat.

After gracing the horses with a few colorful new names and pulling myself upright, I got them calmed down. My blood was boiling, and I was about to bark at Julina when she turned to Lucy and said in an English accent, "It seems this boy you 'ave chosen to escort us on this jaunt has a lot to learn about handling a team." She batted her eyes, and I couldn't keep from laughing.

Lucy lifted the slicker and said, "If you two are finished with your games, I think the slicker will cover us all."

Julina scooted closer. Lucy caught my eye with a knowing smirk.

Julina held the slicker open and said, "Now Taw, my momma taught me to never bite. I promise you don't need to be afraid."

I laughed, and the rest of the way to Salt Lake I held Julina close. I really loved her, and would soon have to make a decision.

I'd have to decide if I was going to ask Julina to marry me. Yet, I doubted she'd consent if I refused to go to church. If I wanted her, I'd have to start living like a Mormon and going to church. Sure, I'd been baptized as a youngun; but I'd never been sure it was the right thing to do. I didn't really feel bad about it, 'til Ma died.

That changed me. If we'd never got baptized, Ma never would have drowned in that river. From that time on, I'd never given church a chance. Was it in me to change, because of a girl?

I might have done a lot of foolish things in my life, but one thing I could never do was to live a lie. I couldn't go to church if I didn't believe. To this point in my life, I didn't believe. But then I was haunted by another thought: If there wasn't anything to being a Mormon, why were Julina, Lucy, Paul, and Lars all so devoted?

Maybe there was something I'd missed. Perhaps I'd quit too soon, hadn't given it a chance. With that thought a kind of peaceful feeling came over me, and it felt good.

I hadn't spoken in quite a while. I'd sat with my arm around Julina, holding her close. The wagon stopped in front of Lucy's new house. I jumped down and hauled Lucy's things inside. Julina had been watching for some time without speaking. When I finished, she took my hand and said softly, "I know you are struggling about the Church. The man I marry will raise our family in the gospel."

It was as if she had been able to read my mind. Then she kissed me.

Julina spent the night at Lucy's house. She planned to stay several days and then ride the train to Sandy City, where her brother would fetch her. The rail line had just been built to Sandy Station. As soon as the loading platform was built, my ore-hauling trips would be cut in half. I could make that trip in two days instead of the four it took to go north to Salt Lake.

On the trip back to Alta, I had plenty to think about. Whenever I thought I should give church another look, a strange feeling settled over me. I felt kind of uneasy. It was a restless feeling that made me feel like there was something I needed to know. It wasn't real strong, but it was always there. After I reached Alta, the thought left me. But on the next long wagon ride, it returned.

These feelings haunted me, but I didn't know what I could do. Maybe I should talk to Paul, but I didn't think I had the nerve. The rest of that fall and winter of 1872, I felt drawn to learn more about the Church—but not like I had back in Pennsylvania. I really wanted to know.

But I didn't do anything about it.

Chapter Ten

I was in love.

I'd known Julina for several years, and had always thought she was as pretty as a spring wild flower. But I never figured to be acting like a lovesick puppy. She was a church-going person, and I wasn't. But I'd fallen about as hard as anybody could. And if that wasn't enough, I knew I'd also started to change, too. I wasn't cussing as much. I spent lots of time thinking about where I would like to farm when I got married. I even thought about going to church! I never mentioned that to anybody, of course. I didn't want my friends to think I'd lost my mind.

That's what was banging around inside of my head on a freezing January morning in 1873. Any winter morning in Alta was cold, but that morning won the prize. Each breath burned my lungs, and when I took my hand out of my glove for more than a few seconds it lost all feeling.

The cold stabbed through my furs and set my teeth to knocking. How I wanted to crawl back between those warm blankets! Instead, I was standing under the roof of my horse shelter, warming the bit for a cantankerous gray gelding.

I built a small fire in an old metal drum and hunched over, warming the bit. Each morning I had to spend a few minutes warming the iron bit and parts of my buckles. They got so cold overnight that they'd stick to bare skin and tear it.

My gray gelding glared at me through half-closed eyes while I hunkered over the fire. He seemed to be daring me to try and ride him on such a miserable morning.

I'd caught him as a colt on the desert. Most mustangs that were young when they were caught tamed down, but this fiery gray had a streak of mean that wouldn't go away. Whenever I tried to saddle him, he'd watch and wait for an opportunity to sink his teeth in me or connect with one of his swift kicks. I'd grown accustomed to his ways, though; and try as he might, I could always keep away from his heels. That just made him all the more ornery.

A fine dusting of powdery snow had sifted through the shingles of the lean-to overnight. With every breath the hairs in my nose stuck together. All feeling had left my cheeks and nose.

I'd lived through a lot of misery with the gray. I told myself a hundred times to get rid of him, but somehow had never got around to it. It was the same way with Alta. Ever since claimjumpers had started killing honest miners, I'd wanted to leave, but I hadn't gotten around to doing it. It was easier to leave things like they were. As dangerous as it was to keep working in Alta, I guess I never thought I might get shot.

The same thing went for Julina. I guess, deep in my mind, I'd finally decided to marry her. I hadn't gotten around to talking myself into it, though. I'd already saved enough for a farm, but kept telling myself that with a little more money I could buy a bigger farm. I'd been telling myself that for a long time.

I wasn't the only one whose mind had been fogged by greed. There was a town full of people who stayed in this frozen hell all winter, all of them wanting to leave but held back by the thought of one last ounce. We were all in the same boat. Everyone hated being here, yet no one could pull themselves away from the silver.

I swung into the saddle, and ducking my head, walked the gray into the chill of the high mountain air. He gave a shudder and danced a might as I headed him down the trail. Except for a light skiff of snow that fell overnight, the snow trail remained hard-packed from the constant travel of sleighs and rawhide tarps used to haul ore.

The sun hadn't begun to gray the sky yet. Moonlight reflected off the new snow like an ocean of twinkling stars. Here and there, stovepipes dotted the flat, snowy field. Alta received huge amounts of snow, and from December to April most of the town was completely buried under a blanket of white. The only signs that shacks were under the snow were the stovepipes and the entryways, where the stairs had been shoveled.

A smoking stovepipe meant there was somebody down there. If the stovepipe wasn't smoking, another swindle might be going on. During the previous winter, a rich-looking sleigh came from the bottom of the canyon with groups of prospectors looking to stake claims. A tall, skinny man with a gray beard was offering cabins for sale at a cheap price. As he walked around on top of the snow, he'd point to a stovepipe and tell the prospector how comfortable the cabin down below was. Most of the prospectors got so excited about the deal they could hardly keep from throwing their money at him.

He walked around and tied a different colored cloth to each stovepipe so that the new owners would know which cabin was theirs. Most of the prospectors never bothered to ask why stairs weren't shoveled down to the cabin—probably because negotiations were conducted over bottles of rye whiskey in one of the saloons. In the spring, the tall, skinny man moved to San Francisco, and the anxious prospectors came to claim their cabins. To their dismay, they found nothing but spring mud connected to the ends of those stovepipes. This didn't stop many of them. They simply found an available piece of ground and built a place or moved into the first vacant shack they found. When the real owners of the property discovered what had happened, many a gunfight ensued. The undertaker made a trip a day to the cemetery at Collins Gulch that spring.

The main part of town sat one hundred yards south of my

shack. The second floors of most buildings were all you could see above the snow. Here and there, stairways had been dug down to ground level; tunnels ran between the busiest saloons and shops. In the winter, Alta became a town of human moles.

Winter snows completely buried the horse sheds. Those of us who kept our horses working in the winter built temporary shelters on top of the snow. It was easier to build shelters near rock walls or in the scattered groves of trees, but this meant the horses stayed a quarter of a mile from our shacks. Mountain lions worked the area, now and then pulling down horses. Some freighters built lean-tos near their stovepipes. This allowed the horses to get out of the wind and falling snow and warm themselves by standing near the warm air rising from the stovepipes. It also kept them away from the hungry cats that hid in the cliffs.

Freighters usually took good care of their horses and made sure they were provided with a good windbreak. But a lot of the miners were blinded with greed, and nothing but silver entered their thoughts. Two miners, unconcerned with the welfare of their animal, foolishly tied their mare out in the open, with no lean-to or windbreak to shelter it. Only warm air rising from the stovepipe had kept the horse from freezing to death.

When I rode past the poor mare on a frosty winter morning and saw the icicles hanging off her coat, I shook my head. I wanted to do something, but in this town you minded your own business if you didn't want to get shot.

On New Year's Eve there was a heavy snowfall. The chilled horse kicked over the stovepipe trying to get warm, and snow drifted over the doorway during the night. The next morning the whole town was so hung over no one noticed. After a few days, somebody got around to shoveling the snow away and found both miners dead. Smoke filled their cabin, and they suffocated. Dying in a cave-in, being buried by an avalanche, or winding up shot by some drunk—Alta was a miserable place. Food and whiskey sellers charged twice the price as purveyors at the canyon mouth. Miners, afraid someone might try to jump their claim, paid high prices rather than make the trip. Life was cheap. Everything else cost plenty.

The first mile down the trail, the gray pulled at the reins, acting mighty uppity. Dancing some, he gave a few crow-hops and settled down. I worried that the fool horse would jump into soft snow and break his leg. I saw spots of blood. A small weasel in its winter-white fur scurried across my path with a mouse in its mouth.

With a fresh coat of snow, the canyon was a sight to behold. The stars faded, and shafts of sunlight lined the sky. The first rays of sunlight struck the high peaks on the north side of the canyon. Peaks rose straight out of the canyon like icy sabres. Here and there I saw the tracks of small snow slides. Over the past few years, logging had cleared all the timber from the canyon bottom. The only trees left were high up on the steep slopes. The dark green of the pines against the white snow and the gray peaks made me stop and stare.

I cursed my job and the filthy town of Alta, but when I was making my trips between Alta and the mouth of the canyon, I was struck with its beauty.

I seldom rode down the canyon on horseback because I usually guided a team on my sleigh. A few days earlier my sleigh had broken a runner, and I'd taken it to Lars. He couldn't haul granite in the winter and was fixing it. Besides, it gave me a reason to drop in on Julina. I was always looking for a reason to do that.

Lars was mighty handy, and when he couldn't haul granite, he made do with odd jobs. He mended harnesses and black-smithed. He found parts for my sleigh in Salt Lake, so during the few days I couldn't work, I helped another freighter haul supplies back to Alta. Heading back to pick up my sleigh, I'd soon begin my endless string of trips.

During the months when the snow was the deepest, the teamsters hauled the ore down the canyon in sleighs or on green hide slips. After the heaviest storms, a sleigh could make it all the way to the rail head at Sandy Station. Most of the time sleighs stopped at the mouth of the canyon and substituted wheels for runners before continuing to Sandy. The rawhided ore was loaded onto wagons at the canyon mouth. At Sandy Station the ore was loaded onto train cars and headed to San Francisco, then shipped around the Horn to Wales. Even after all of this, the ore still brought the owners of the mines a tidy profit.

Demand seemed never-ending. Mining continued even in the worst weather. When the weather was the worst, the ore would pile up in the mouths of the mines. With warmer weather, mine owners became desperate to haul the excess away so mining wouldn't stop. After haggling over price, the trips I took down the canyon became very profitable. If a mine owner didn't offer what I thought the market could bear, I threatened to haul for another mine equally as desperate. I received twice the normal wages of company freighters. Winter months lined my pockets with silver.

The last several months I worked exclusively for the Emma mine, the mine that made Alta. She still produced an endless stream of the richest ore this country had seen.

As cold as the canyon became, the risk of getting caught and freezing to death in a blizzard didn't scare me. If temperatures dropped too low, I jumped off the wagon and built a snow cave and sat out the storm.

The real danger loomed in avalanches.

Each afternoon a heavy fog billowed up the canyon. The wind would pick up and drive falling snow into the face of anyone heading down the canyon. New fallen snow with high winds is what usually triggered the slides. With fog cutting vision and wind muffling any sound, a slide could bury an unlucky teamster without him being aware it was coming.

Each winter, men and teams disappeared. The following spring somebody would find their bodies where tons of snow had buried them. We knew the danger and were careful since we traveled the same trails every day. All of us had seen dozens of avalanches charging down the hillsides. We tried to avoid areas that posed the greatest risk, but as careful as we were, more than one freighter lost his life each winter.

The day after the Christmas of 1872, an enormous slide roared down Hellgate ravine near the Emma mine. Eleven sleighs were trapped. An army of men rushed out of the saloons and mines to help in the rescue. Three men were dug out alive. Six were found dead—four never were found.

The day after a heavy snowstorm was usually the riskiest. I'd often see a dozen or more slides charging down the canyon walls on those days. Where the slides covered the trail, we teamsters would spend whatever time necessary to clear it.

To stay alive in this canyon, you had to travel quietly, moving quickly across open slopes, stopping in the thickest timber, and always watching the mountain above you. A rabbit's foot in your pocket didn't hurt either.

The going had been particularly slow this morning. The ride down the trail made me wish I'd sold the gray. Small slides covered the trail in half a dozen places. A large slide covered a quarter mile of the trail. I stopped to help another freighter cut away a fallen tree. I worked up a good sweat and removed my furs in the process.

We finished about noon. I changed out of my sweaty clothes and put my furs back on. A good way to die in this canyon was to work up a sweat and not change your clothes. When you stopped working, the sweat would freeze against your skin. Soon you started stumbling and acting drunk. Next you might sit down and go to sleep, never waking up. I didn't plan to die that way. I always carried spare clothes when traveling in the winter.

I climbed back onto the saddle. The gray seemed anxious to get down the canyon; he knew that grain and a warm stall awaited him. A mile further I topped a small rise. A half mile down the canyon to my left, I saw the group of buildings called Tanner. Tanner wasn't really a town. It was just a group of cabins and shacks that were next to each other. It started around a small saw mill, but last summer a fire made that a memory. A small smelting operation had located itself there, but because it was in constant disrepair it never prospered.

Most of the other people who lived in Tanner cut timber in the canyon. Timber milled in the canyon found its way into the mines as supports. Some lumber traveled to the valley or became charcoal. Several Mormon freighters lived in Tanner, but most lived further down the canyon at Granite. The snow depth in Tanner never approached the depth in Alta, just four miles up the canyon. The snow piled around the cabins, but it never completely covered them up.

Suddenly, the calm of the day was shattered by a gunshot from across the valley. Reigning in the gray and putting my hand up to my eyes, I found where the shot had come from. I saw a man standing near a horse and pointing to something in the deep snow. I could make out a deer. He must have been a lousy shot, because the deer was only one hundred yards from him and still alive. Another shot boomed and echoed down the canyon. The deer fell still.

I shook my head in disgust. At this time of year, any deer at this altitude would be a sack of skin and bones at best.

Gazing across the canyon, I suddenly sensed something else.

The sound of the gunshot had died a couple of seconds before, yet I still heard a deep rumbling. Panicking, I jerked my head around and looked up at the slope behind me. The entire mountainside above me was moving in one enormous avalanche! I jammed my spurs into the gray, and he leapt toward an island of pines a quarter of a mile down the trail. I prided myself in being careful with snowslides, yet I'd committed the gravest of sins when traveling in steep, snowy country. I'd stopped in the middle of a large, open hillside. This moment of carelessness might now cost me my life. The wall of snow and ice churning toward me swallowed everything in its path. I could see an enormous cloud of fine snow kick up in front of the avalanche as it charged down the long hillside.

Hunched over my horse, I hoped his footing would remain firm and he wouldn't step into any soft snow and go down. The gray sensed the urgency and gave the sprint everything he had. His breath came in steamy bursts as his legs churned wildly toward the trees. The hillside shook from the wall of ice and snow.

I covered over three quarters of the distance. The grove of trees loomed, and for the first time I felt hope. Just two more strides! I glimpsed up at the moving wall of ice, and the white mist of powdered snow engulfed me. I felt a rush of icy wind, and with the trees just fifty feet away, the gray stumbled and slammed against the side of my body. It was as if somebody had hit me with a board. Vaguely I heard the gray scream, and then I knew.

The avalanche had caught me, and I found myself being swept toward the canyon bottom. I fought to stay on the surface. I tried to swim with the flow. One moment I'd find myself looking into the blue sky, the next I was tumbled and buried. The snow, littered with rocks, ice, and tree branches, battered me as I tumbled along. Time and again I fought my way to the surface, and each time I was swallowed up by the charging mass of snow and ice.

I struck my head, and everything went black.

Chapter Eleven

I struggled to regain consciousness. My head throbbed, and I felt a sharp pain above my left ear. My body ached everywhere, yet I felt strangely warm. I couldn't move my hand to the ache on the side of my head. My face was pushed into something . . . something cold. My mouth was full of snow. With a start, I remembered.

In a blind panic, I began to thrash about. I tried to fight my way to freedom. With all my struggles, I could barely move. I was buried in snow! My frantic movements met with firm resistance everywhere. My thrashing did slightly enlarge the cocoon surrounding me, but not enough to allow me to move freely. Finally, exhausted, I stopped struggling and tried to control my heavy breathing. I knew that I must subdue my panic if I was to have any chance of escape. I'd been in tight spots in the past, and I knew that if I didn't keep a clear head now, I'd die.

I decided to lie still and think through my predicament. I lay on my stomach with my left arm extended beyond my head and bent at the elbow, my hand near my ear. My right arm was twisted behind my back. My shoulder throbbed and felt like it was broken. My knees were drawn up to my chest.

I had just enough room to move my head. Using my left hand, I pushed snow away from the front of my face. I created a small cavity that I could breathe into. The surrounding snow was firm, but not frozen solid. I would be able to breathe the air trapped in the snow until my breath made a sheet of ice of the snow near my face. Then I would slowly suffocate. But the snow surrounding my head was still soft enough to allow me to push it aside with my left hand. After several minutes I dug a bowl around my face the size of a bread basket.

Pushing with my feet, I was able to slide into the space I'd dug. This let me straighten my legs slightly. As I slid forward, I freed my right arm behind me. With great effort, I was able to work my right hand to my face. My shoulder throbbed, but I could use my arm, so I figured it wasn't broken.

A terrifying thought came to me. Each winter, men were caught in avalanches in this canyon. Many of the men buried were dug out before they died, but the ones who lived were usually traveling with someone who saw where they were buried. If the rescuers found them in time, they typically were no worse for the experience. I'd heard those men speak of becoming lightheaded as they used up their air. They would suck air in gasping breaths as it was nearly used up. If the rescue took too long, the buried teamster would be found with the gasp of his last breath frozen on his face.

Another thought struck fear into my heart. I traveled alone. No one would be nearby to look for me! But the people in Tanner would see the slide and should investigate. There was a small hope someone would find me. But I knew that if no clear sign of where I was buried could be found, my chances of being found alive were slim.

Fear seized me, and I thought I would certainly die. I'd slowly suffocate until in one painful gasp, I lost consciousness. In a panic, I began to thrash about within the confines of the tiny burrow. In moments I had to stop, because my breath came in heaving gasps.

As my breathing slowed, I told myself that my struggles weren't going to do me any good. I again told myself that I needed to use my head if I was to have any hope of survival.

With that thought, I relaxed and tried to think of a way out.

Ma always taught me to pray when I faced problems. When I was a young boy, we prayed as a family every night. After Ma became a Mormon, prayer took on an even more important part in my family.

When I was a kid I used to pray with my family, but by myself I didn't have much luck. I tried to be good, but as a young boy, unless my mother looked on, I usually fell asleep or couldn't control my hunger long enough to remember my prayers. After Ma died I couldn't pray anymore, and I hadn't said a prayer since that day. Now, as hopeless as my situation seemed, I couldn't bring myself to say a prayer.

I've no idea how long I lay there in thought. I might have fallen asleep, because I felt groggy and had to shake myself to regain my senses. My cheek had lost all feeling from lying in the cold snow, and the snow under my face had turned to a sheet of ice.

Punching the snow above my head in frustration, I found that it was soft. My fist penetrated several inches. Using both hands, I excavated a bucket-sized hole ahead of me. My legs, still bent, were cramping miserably. Then, wriggling like a worm, I worked myself forward until my head touched the far end of the hole I had just made. I straightened out my legs to relieve the cramping.

Soft snow was now under my face, and breathing became easier. I felt myself start to panic again, and it took everything I could muster to keep my head. The beating of my heart seemed to fill the cavity with a hypnotic pulse. With each movement, icy tingles danced on my back and neck.

I heard crunching sounds and felt a vibration. It took a few moments before I realized what it was—somebody walking on the snow above me!

I immediately began to yell and pound the snow, but the footsteps were receding. I clawed at the snow above my face like a man possessed, but my frantic breathing had frozen it solid, and my flailing just injured my already bruised hands. It took a few moments after the sound vanished before I stopped. What hope I had left was wrenched from my soul. I felt warm tears running over my chilled cheeks. What fairness existed here? Why should I die? Wasn't Alta filled with people more deserving of death than I was?

I settled back and peered into the inky, frozen blackness. Death could not be far off now. I'd lie here and calmly drift off into sleep, never waking up. They'd never even know what happened to me. Julina would never . . .

I awoke with a start. I had drifted into sleep. My furs had kept me warm, but for the first time I noticed my feet were losing feeling. A thought struck me—why ain't I dead? I didn't know how long I'd been buried, but it seemed like days.

How it began, I can't really say; but without any conscious act of my own, I found myself talking to God for the first time since I could remember. My prayer came simply and haltingly. It probably wasn't much of a prayer, but being out of practice as I was, it was all I could do. When I ended, I felt the same goosebumpy feeling I had first felt when I'd been taught by the Mormon Elders. A calmness spread over me, my heart stopped pounding, and suddenly I no longer feared death.

As I lay there, I remembered something. I worked my hand down my side and found the large bowie knife I always wore. I worked my hand back up and brought the knife up to my face. I tried to tap at the snow in front of me, but my breath had turned it into an icy sheet. The snow held my arm tightly to my body, so I couldn't swing the knife with enough force to break through the ice. In frustration, I stabbed the knife directly above my head. My arm had enough freedom to allow me to jab. My breath had not frozen all the snow, and my knife penetrated easily. Chiseling and chopping, I began to dig. After several minutes, I found I had dug out a pocket as far as I could reach. Like a worm, I gingerly slithered into the cavity.

I kept on digging. I hadn't any plan, but I knew I had to stay active. With the knife I made slow, constant progress. Every few minutes I wiggled further into the hole I'd cleared.

I might be able to tunnel out. I also thought I might be heading deeper into the snow. But I figured the only chance I had was to keep digging, and I prayed I was tunneling toward the surface.

My effort to tunnel made me realize how chilled my feet were. I'd lost all feeling in them, but now they were stabbed with chillblains.

I encountered a large tree trunk. I tunneled beneath it and found that the bows had not allowed the snow to pack firmly. What snow was in between the branches was loosely packed and gave way easily. My shoulders ached and my back was stiff from the digging, yet I continued on, too fearful to rest.

Wiggling under the tree trunk, I found myself tumbling into a large cavity crisscrossed with a maze of boughs and branches—and a large air pocket which had formed underneath. I reasoned that if I followed the trunk to the top, I should eventually escape.

The snow was light and easy to push out of the way. I wormed between branches and sensed freedom. I hadn't realized I'd tunneled free until a breeze blew powdery snow in my face. Looking through the maze of branches, I saw a few twinkling stars between the high clouds. I crawled from the tangle of branches and collapsed in the open snow. I wanted to shout with joy.

I had escaped.

How many times had I felt I would never see a star twinkle again? I had no idea how long I'd been buried in that icy tomb, but I was free at last. I paused and wondered. Was my prayer answered? Did I do it all myself?

As I knelt in the snow, I thought back to just a few hours earlier. I'd given up. I was ready to close my eyes and never wake up. There was no way out, and I was sure I'd soon be dead.

But something happened. After I'd given up hope and was sure I was going to die, I prayed. As soon as I was through, the thought to dig came to my mind. Was that an answer to my prayer? As I wondered, a warmness came to me. It felt so peaceful and nice. Then I remembered: years before, I'd felt the same way when the Elders first taught my family. Maybe this was the way prayers were answered.

How long I knelt in the snow, I didn't know. I didn't want the feelings to leave. The wind picked up and a chill came to me again. But before I stood up, I bowed my head and offered a quiet thank-you.

I climbed to my numbed feet. I touched my cheeks; I'd been crying, but I hadn't noticed. Limping, I set my course onward for Tanner.

Chapter Twelve

I stayed in Tanner for a week. My feet had gotten so cold that the skin had turned black and started peeling off. For a few days they were so swollen that I couldn't put on my boots. But that had passed. I could at least walk now, though it pained me plenty.

I picked up my sleigh from Lars and drove it back to Alta. As the horses headed up the canyon, clouds blocked the sun and the wind chilled me through. The trail remained hard-packed, since no snow had fallen in several days. I passed several sleighs heading down the canyon; each of the drivers greeted me, asking about the avalanche. Word had spread everywhere about how I'd tunneled out of the slide.

I arrived at the lean-to where I kept my horses and unloaded the hay, grain, and supplies I'd brought from the canyon mouth. I unhitched the team and forked hay in their manger, then dug out the snow from the entrance to my shack and built a fire in the old metal stove.

My shack appeared as I'd left it: an old, rusted metal bed with my bedroll, a chest to keep my things in, and a small table with two stumps serving as chairs. I stowed my extra food and guns. The pistol, an old dragoon piece, became mine when Pa died. It was a big gun, weighing almost five pounds when loaded. My rifle was a Sharps .53 caliber, the best gun made.

I warmed up by the fire, put away my gear, and then climbed the stairs to the surface of the snow and wandered to the main part of town. The wind picked up and a light snowfall began. Misty gray clouds crept up the canyon from the valley below. My skin tightened and my eyelashes stuck together at the touch of the icy wind. I quickened my steps, hoping to get inside as quickly as possible.

I hurried down Walker Street, the only real street in Alta. I saw the top floor of the Grand Hotel rising out of the snow. The depth of the snowpack made it possible to look into the windows of the second floor. Across the street from where I stood, Joe Brandy's Restaurant and Bar stuck up from the snow. Here and there, assorted roof ridges and second floors could be seen, marking other saloons and restaurants.

At the far end of the street, five tall pine trees stood guard. These were some of the last trees in the bottom of the canyon. Lumbering had cleared all the other trees. A set of stairs cut into the snow allowed entrance to the hotel. This year, like many earlier years, the snow was so deep that miners moved through the tunnels connecting the hotel with several saloons. During the last two years, traffic to the cemetery at Collins Gulch had also kept a tunnel clear during the winter.

I didn't find anybody in the hotel. The girls hadn't started dancing yet, and whiskey cost less at Brandy's. I went next door to the billiard hall. Mr. Fitzgerald ran the place. He was a miserable little man who never had anything nice to say. Tobacco juice always stained his chin, and I'd never seen him change his shirt. He insisted that everyone call him Mr. Fitzgerald. What he lacked in size he made up in obnoxiousness. The few teeth in his mouth were stained brown; he had a rough, gravelly voice; and he was always quick to grab for a shotgun whenever a couple of drunks got a little noisy.

Waves of heat hit me as I entered the room. It always seemed crowded and filthy, with tobacco stains and cigar butts on the floor. Two billiard tables crowded the small floor, and patrons were constantly bumping into each other while trying to play. This led to many arguments.

A couple of weeks earlier, I had been playing at one table when two miners, Tex Hendricks and Les McCarty, got into an argument. Tex spat tobacco juice onto the table where I was playing with McCarty. I knew Tex's reputation and froze, but McCarty had been drinking and swung at him. Tex ducked and threw a chair at McCarty. McCarty then broke a pool cue over Tex's back.

I didn't want any of this trouble, so I stayed out of the way. Mr. Fitzgerald pulled out his shotgun and told them to get the hell out or he'd make sure the undertaker dragged them out.

Tex, who had started out the door, grabbed and jerked the barrel of Fitzgerald's gun as he passed. The gun discharged, sending buckshot slamming into McCarty's right hip and knocking him to the floor. Tex turned and sneered at the dying McCarty, "That's the last fight you'll ever pick." He then walked out the door. A couple of us took McCarty over to the doc's place. The doc seemed to be more interested in who was going to pay him than in helping McCarty. We finally talked him into putting a poultice on McCarty's hip, and the doc said he would be back in a couple of hours to change it. He walked to the Grand Hotel, got interested in the dancing girls, and forgot.

The next morning when he returned, McCarty was dead. It seemed that Tex had intended the shot to go off and hit McCarty, but an argument could be made for it being an accident. Nobody was going to arrest Hendricks without a gunfight—and as handy as he was with his guns, nobody was too interested in trying.

I left Fitzgerald's place and walked down the snow tunnel to Brandy's. It buzzed with activity. Several teamsters gathered around a table, and when I entered they waved me over to their table. I told them my avalanche story. They just shook their heads. None of them ever heard of someone tunneling out of an avalanche.

They filled me in on the gossip I had missed in the last few days. Word on the streets was that the Emma was in trouble. It seemed the Englishmen who'd bought the mine were on their way to look into the matter. Most of the teamsters figured that some sort of swindle had taken place. In the last few days, most of the miners who had been working the Emma had left town. But I didn't let it bother me. There were always more miners, and I didn't care who owned the Emma as long as I kept busy hauling the ore.

I looked around the room; men were gambling at a couple of the tables. My lips tightened when I saw Tex Hendricks sitting at the table nearest us. He stood over six feet tall, and he had a coldness in his eyes that made my skin crawl. His gray eyes were close together and constantly moving from side to side. He wore a big red mustache and sideburns, but had lost most of his hair on top.

Though playing cards, Tex seemed to be trying to hear what we were talking about. Rico Juarez, one of the men who worked in his mine, sat next to him. Half Mexican and half Paiute, he wore his long, greasy hair tied in back. His face was marked with several scars. When he grinned, you could see his two front teeth were missing.

Rico stood under six feet tall, had a slender build, and would just as soon shoot you as look at you. Tex had a reputation for killing several men, but I suspected Rico might sometimes have pulled the trigger. Rico and Tex were inseparable. They both worked the same mine, yet never hauled out much ore. They had money to spend, though. The whisperings around town blamed them for several holdups in the canyon and at Silver Fork, the next canyon over. The holdups had been pulled by two masked men. They had always gotten away, and their tracks never left the canyon.

The outlaws had first hit the payroll on the stagecoach that ran up the canyon from Salt Lake. Since the stage line countered by sending two armed men inside along with the driver, the stage had been left alone. Most of the other holdups had been of lone men who were foolish enough to ride down the canyon with large sums of money on them.

Tex had earned quite a reputation. Besides killing McCarty, a few years earlier he had acquired the claim he was working in a gunfight with the original claim holder. Tex moved onto the claim when the man left to visit his family. Upon returning and finding someone else working his claim, the miner faced Tex at the saloon. An argument ensued, and the miner threatened with, "Get off the claim or else."

The miner left the saloon. Tex followed a moment later, and two shots boomed outside. The saloon emptied and the miner lay on the ground with a smoking revolver in his hand. Hendricks stood nearby with his revolver already holstered.

Rico claimed to have seen the whole thing. The miner had waited for Tex behind the dry goods store. As Tex had come by, the miner had stepped out and fired. Tex, catching the movement out of the corner of his eye, had dodged and returned the shot. The miner died before he hit the ground. No one else had witnessed the killing, so Rico's testimony stood. At the time, Rico had not been known to associate with Tex.

The miner's widow came to town a couple of days later and had raised disturbing questions with the deputy. She claimed her husband didn't own a revolver. When she wanted to see the pistol, the deputy couldn't find it. The sheriff promised to look into the matter, but once she left town nothing happened.

Since then, Tex had been involved in several gunfights, but the only witnesses seemed to be Rico or some other associate of Tex's. Their testimonies always stated that Tex acted in self-defense. That disturbed many people, but the sheriff never seemed to be interested in prying too deeply.

I was leaving the saloon when Hendricks tapped me from behind. "Stoner," he said, "come over to my mine tomorrow. I have some ore I want hauled down the canyon."

Turning around, I looked into his dark, narrow eyes. I had no desire to haul ore for him, yet I didn't want to start trouble.

I began to speak when Hendricks cut in, "Don't try to give

me any excuses. I overheard you, and I know you haven't made arrangements to haul anyone else's ore."

I knew I couldn't show weakness with this lowlife. "All right Tex," I asked, "how much are you paying?"

Hendricks answered, "Ten dollars a ton."

Nobody paid that much. I knew he was up to something, but I couldn't turn him down; that would invite a fight. "All right, I'll be there before sunup. Don't make me wait."

Hendricks said, "Bring your sleigh over tonight, and we'll have it loaded by the time you get there." He threw his long, skinny cigar into the snow and disappeared down the snow tunnel. When I rode to the mine with my sleigh, I found Rico waiting near a fire. I asked him where he wanted me to leave the sleigh, and he pointed without answering. His flat, expressionless eyes gazed at me and made my stomach knot. I unhitched the sorrel mare and turned her back toward my shack. I couldn't help but wonder why Rico and Hendricks would pay ten dollars a ton to have their ore hauled when anybody in town would haul it for eight. Something about this entire situation didn't feel right, and I didn't want to work for these two no matter how much they paid.

An idea came to me. I'd go and arrange to begin hauling for the Emma mine as soon as I returned from hauling Hendricks' load. That way I could haul this one load but someone else could haul the rest of their ore. I'd have an excuse so I wouldn't have to haul more than the one load. I turned my horse and began to look for the foreman of the Emma.

Early the next morning I brought my team to the sleigh. Rico and Hendricks were warming themselves near a fire. Hendricks wore a large buffalo coat, and Rico wore a slicker like the one I owned. They offered me a cup of coffee, and after I poured I looked into the back of the sleigh. The sleigh was only half full. I turned and said, "What's the problem here? You said the sleigh would be loaded and ready to go. It's only half full."

Hendricks said coolly while blowing on his coffee, "That's all you're taking."

Angrily I said, "You hired me to haul a full load. I don't take partial loads."

Hendricks replied without looking up from his coffee, "We're paying for a full load."

I looked at Hendricks in stunned silence. "Pay me now," I said.

Hendricks motioned to Rico, who pulled three twenty-dollar gold pieces from his pocket and threw them into the snow in front of me. I picked up the coins and dropped them into my pocket. I threw the coffee grounds out into the snow and dropped the cup next to the fire, then I hitched the team and jumped into my seat. Hendricks still hadn't moved. He just squatted in front of the fire, sipping his coffee. I prepared to slap the team when Rico jumped into the seat next to me. He looked at me with his reptile-like eyes and said, "Protecting my investment."

I began to protest and Hendricks said, "You've been paid. Just shut up and go."

I felt my face flush, and I gripped the reins tightly in my fist. I knew I had to be careful with these two. I smiled at Hendricks and said, "Tex, I'll enjoy the conversation."

I whipped the team and set off down the canyon. The clear sky foretold a sunny day. I checked under my seat for the pair of colored glasses I kept to protect my eyes from the sun. I noticed my slicker folded under the seat.

With the light load, we reached the granite quarry in no time at all. Rico stared ahead, never saying a word. As we reached the quarry, he grabbed the reins from me and stopped the team. He told me to get off the wagon. He would take the load to Sandy Station by himself. My first inclination drove me to protest, but then I thought I'd have a chance to visit with Julina while he delivered the ore to the rail depot.

We agreed to meet the following day at the same time, and I hopped off the sleigh. As I turned to jump from the wagon, I noticed there was something peculiar about the load of ore. It wasn't until he drove off that I realized something beneath the ore had begun to show through as the ore settled. I wondered what they were up to. But I figured it was none of my business, so I walked towards the row of shacks, looking for Paul.

Chapter Thirteen

Paul's primary job at the granite quarry was to select the proper stone and split it into various sizes. He was teamed with the chief stone mason, and at one time or another had done every job at the quarry. I found him playing checkers in the cook house. The weather was still too cold to begin cutting rock. Snow covered most of the ground, but some men worked making tools and repairing wagons. I asked Paul, "Do you have a horse I can use until tomorrow?"

Paul asked, "What for?"

I answered, "My wagon won't be back from Sandy until tomorrow, and I'm planning on staying in Emmaville overnight."

I could tell by the look he gave me that he knew I was planning to visit Julina. Paul called on a couple of girls from time to time, but he didn't seem to be real interested in either of them.

"Sure," he said. "You can ride the steel dust stud." The small stud was a four-year-old. Paul had caught him on the west desert. He had been saddle-broken, but like most desert-born studs, it took a horseman to stay astride him.

I hurried to the corral and threw on a saddle. I jumped on and the young horse bucked and jumped for a few minutes. Determined to not let him unseat me, I finally headed him to Emmaville.

Emmaville was a town that never worked out. It started as a midway point for teamsters to spend the night who were hauling ore from Alta to Salt Lake. With the grade to Alta being too steep, a wagon couldn't make the trip from Emmaville to Alta in one day.

Land promoters tried to get the railroad to come through Emmaville on the way to the mouth of the canyon, but it went to Sandy City instead. With that, all the ore freighters left town and moved to Granite. The granite freighters still drove through Emmaville, but that too would end later when the railroad extended to the mouth of canyon. Soon, there wouldn't be much of a town left.

Lars still made his home there. But I wasn't going to see Lars. I hadn't seen Julina in several weeks, and I missed her. Almost every boy in this part of the valley had called on her at one time or another, but what bothered me was that Jed Mathews saw her whenever she went to St. George.

I knew she had received marriage proposals, and so far she had turned everyone down. Lucy told me she was waiting for me. I had dreamed about marrying Julina, but I just wasn't ready.

Lucy told me Julina wouldn't wait forever, and if I loved her I should make up my mind. Julina's father, being aware of our mutual interest, did not approve of his daughter marrying a lukewarm Mormon. To keep us apart, he would send her to St. George as often as possible to stay with her sister. I think he hoped she would lose interest in me.

I had been thinking about what Lucy had said. If I loved Julina, I had to decide if I wanted to start getting religion or not. Her devotion to her religion ran deep. I knew she wouldn't marry me if I refused to go to church. I couldn't kid myself. I could never become a church-going Mormon unless I believed in it. So, if I embraced the Church, I couldn't do it for Lars or Lucy or Julina. I had to do it for myself. With all these thoughts swimming in my head, I rode up to the Smith place and noticed a fancy carriage out front.

I knocked on the door of the large, two-story house. One of

Julina's younger brothers let me in. Children swarmed up the stairs like invading locusts. I had no idea how many wives or children Orson Smith had, but he could field a small army.

I entered the parlor and my jaw almost fell off. Sitting on a wooden bench was Jed Mathews. I felt the blood pounding in my ears, and my muscles tightened all over. He glared when he saw me, but looked away when Julina entered the room.

She looked about as pretty as a girl could get in her ruffled blue dress. Jed stood up and greeted Julina graciously, and then she looked at me, smiled, and said, "Taw, it is so nice to see you. I would like to introduce you to Jed Mathews. His father runs cattle in St. George."

I answered, "I've met Jed before."

Jed answered, "We've met. We were in the same wagon company coming West."

"Julina, did he tell you how he would steal my supper, force me to do his work, and try to beat me up whenever he could?" I turned to Jed and continued, "I also remember you had a loud mouth and were despised by nearly everyone."

Jed flushed, and I added, "By the way, Jed, did you ever tell Julina about the picnic?"

Jed began to squirm. I was enjoying myself. I had forgotten about why I had come for the visit, and I found myself wanting to grab him by his skinny neck and drag him outside. But Julina brought me to my senses. "Taw, I am surprised at you. Jed's a gentleman. His father is one of the wealthiest ranchers in all of St. George. I think you owe him an apology."

"What?" I almost shouted. "The only thing I owe him is my fist in his mouth."

I was seething, and both Jed and Julina could see it. Then Orson Smith stepped into the room. He didn't say a thing. He just glared at me.

Jed stepped up to him and put out his hand. "My father sends his best wishes to you, Brother Smith. The bull he bought from you is one of the finest he's seen. You should be proud of being the owner of the finest stock in the territory."

Chapter Fourteen

I gritted my teeth. There he was, buttering up the adults. I wish Orson Smith knew what he was really like.

"Thank you, Jed. Your father has done well to raise such a polite son," Orson Smith answered. Turning to me, he continued, "I hope you will remember to keep a civil tongue while a guest in my home."

Julina whispered, "Taw, I must ask you to show more respect for my guest."

"Julina, I'm surprised you can stand to be seen with this snake." With that, I turned and stomped to the door.

As I approached the door, I turned to speak to Julina. Jed gave me a pompous grin. I bit my lip and ducked outside. I jumped onto the steel dust and shot out of the yard. The sun had sunk below the western hills. Darkness extending its black fingers made it difficult to see the trail. But I didn't care. The stud wouldn't stumble.

On and on we raced. I enjoyed the smooth stride and the feeling of the young horse's rippling muscles beneath me. The horse, too, seemed to take great pleasure in this race. It was early spring, and though the snow stood deep at Alta, there were just patches of snow on the frozen ground. Finally, some sense returned to me, and I slowed the stud to a walk. Even though the air was crisp, the steel dust had worked up a considerable lather. He was still raring to go. He pulled at the reins and danced, but finally slowed to a steady walk.

I wandered the foothills for the next few hours. Jed Mathews made me wild with jealousy. I pondered my feelings for Julina. Did I really love her? Did I want to get married now? Would she marry me? My head swam. Half a dozen times I decided to forget her. I reasoned that I could always find a girl. Then I decided I couldn't stand never seeing her again.

Why was it that people couldn't see the real Jed? I remembered how Bishop Spiers, from the wagon train, thought Jed was well brought-up, and he didn't believe Jed would bully us younger boys. He also fooled Orson Smith, who was all smiles when Jed was courting Julina. But whenever I showed up, Orson looked like he'd just taken a big swallow of buttermilk. He didn't hide his feelings about me courting Julina.

Jed even had Julina under his spell. Jed just knew the right things to say. He had all kinds of people thinking he was next in line for Brother Brigham's job. Yet the real Jed was a low-down snake.

On the other hand, I was always saying the wrong thing. It just got everybody angry at me. Because of that, everyone thought he was an angel and I was no good.

Hours after midnight, I rode up to Lars' place. I stabled the horse, grabbed up a handful of hay, and rubbed the stud down. Then, rather than wake anybody in the house, I climbed into the loft and made a bed in the straw. In a few hours it would be Sunday morning, and I'd decided to do something I hadn't done in a long time.

Bright and early the next morning, I awoke to the sound of milk squirting into a pail. One of my step-brothers was milking. He hollered up at me and told me if I wanted breakfast I'd better get moving. Walking through the door, I saw Sarah nursing a baby and preparing breakfast.

She greeted me warmly. "It's great to see you, Taw. Join the youngsters before the food's all gone."

They'd already blessed it. The younger children were attacking the mountains of home-fried potatoes and flapjacks like hungry wolves. The Swensen household had grown over the last few years, and the dining table couldn't seat the entire family at once. The younger children ate first while a couple of the older daughters served. The older children ate next, and finally the adults. By the time the third shift finished eating, it was nearly time to start preparing lunch.

Lars had taken a second wife, Inga. She had joined the Church and come from Denmark at age twenty-two. After arriving in the valley with no husband, she went to work helping in the Swensens' home. A year later, she became a plural wife of Lars. The most common way for men to take plural wives seemed to be to marry a woman who helped in their home. With more women than men immigrating to the valley, this happened often.

While Sarah cooked, Inga helped the children dress for church. Lars crashed around upstairs, and it sounded as if a wrestling match was underway. I finished breakfast and walked outside to the loft.

Paul usually spent Sunday here. His clean shirts and shaving gear were stored on a shelf. I cleaned up and put on one of the shirts. The sleeves were too short, so I rolled them up. I brushed off my pants as best I could, shaved, and combed my hair. I saddled the steel dust and sneaked to the side of the barn. I didn't want to explain where I planned to go. I gave the steel dust a slap and cantered down the road.

As I was riding, a sick feeling hit me in the stomach. I hadn't been to a church meeting for so long, I didn't know if I could go through with it. Several times I almost turned and headed back. Why go to church? I knew Lars, Paul, and Julina would be happy to see me, but that had never been enough motivation for me to go in the past. For the first time in my life, I wanted to know if I believed in the Mormon Church. Was Brigham Young really a prophet, or a fraud like all the miners in Alta thought? I didn't know a better way to find out than to go.

As I rode, the thought of walking through the door of the ward house gave me the shivers. I knew that when I entered through the door of the Granite Ward, everyone would stare. I could just guess the thoughts in their minds: "The second coming must be near at hand for Taw Stoner to finally come to church." I knew everyone in the ward, but they'd never seen me here. They knew how I felt. As I came within sight of the ward house, I reined in the stud and almost put my heels to him and galloped away. With a big swallow, I headed him toward the fence next to the front door. Maybe I could sneak in and sit way in the back. Maybe no one would notice me.

It was worse than I'd imagined. As soon as I walked through the door, the bishop, wide-eyed, rushed over and took my hand. "Taw, it's so nice to see you." He asked me a few questions about my work and, turning to the next person to enter, said, "Look who has come to join us today!"

He introduced me to several people who walked through the door. I could tell by the shocked looks that no one expected me. But they were friendly. One of our neighbors said, "Won't Paul be surprised."

That made me want to hide my head. I could imagine Paul's comments. He'd never believe I came to church without being forced. He'd wonder at first if I'd lost a bet. Then he might figure Julina refused to see me anymore if I didn't go.

The bishop stayed next to me and made sure everyone shook my hand. I felt like the fat lady at a circus. I wanted to slink to the back of the chapel and be ignored, but all these friendly people wouldn't leave me alone.

The meeting began and everyone took a seat. Paul walked through the door. I'd promised to have his horse back by early this morning, and he'd walked to church.

He approached me, and with a smirk on his face said, "You make a habit of coming to church, and I'll bet the bishop lets you give a talk." I almost ran out the door.

I found a seat, and the meeting started. As the first hymn was being sung, a couple entered. It was Julina accompanied by

Jed Mathews. I felt like a hot tea kettle before it starts to whistle. They walked up to the front of the chapel. I didn't think Julina had noticed me.

Throughout the meeting I tried to listen to the speaker; but every time I looked over and saw Julina with Jed, I felt the veins in my neck stick out. At one point during the meeting, she rested her head on his shoulder and I felt my face flush. Paul watched my reaction and seemed amused. When all the meetings were over, everyone shook my hand again. Many people told me they hoped to see me again next Sunday. Aside from being embarrassed, it did feel good that they were concerned.

As I walked out the door, Julina met me. Her green eyes sparkled and my heart melted when she smiled. She had left Jed in the carriage and came back to speak to me. She said, "You're the last person I expected to see here today."

I blushed all over again and kicked the dirt when I replied, "Well, I didn't have nothing else to do."

Still smiling, she said, "Taw, I would like to talk to you. Could you meet me in an hour at the cottonwood grove on Willow Creek?"

I said I would, and she gave my hand a little squeeze and left. She ran back to her carriage.

An hour later I waited on the bank of Willow Creek. It was a beautiful sunny day, warm and clear. The trees were alive with songbirds squabbling back and forth. The spring grasses had just started to green the meadows, and the buds on the cottonwoods were swollen and ready to burst open. Snow lingered in the shade of the tall trees.

Julina, pretty as ever, rode up sidesaddle with a blanket and two large saddlebags. I helped her off her horse. At first I felt uncomfortable and didn't know what to say.

She melted my defense and soon had me laughing and talking. She had packed a picnic lunch, and I helped her set it out. We ate and talked, and I lost track of the time. I wasn't just attracted to her pretty face and nice figure—Julina made everything she did fun. Smart, funny, and cute all at the same time. I couldn't ask for more. The time passed too quickly, and before I knew it, I had to help Julina pack away the blanket and dishes so she could return.

As I finished tying on the blanket, I turned away from her horse and she stood close to me. Looking into my eyes, she took my hand and said, "I'm returning to St. George tomorrow. My sister still needs my help." She paused. "Jed is going to accompany me there."

I felt my pulse quicken. I tried to speak, when she said, "He is handsome."

I jumped in, "He's not."

She smiled. "His father is wealthy, too. Someday he'll own his share."

I couldn't tell if she was serious or teasing. I answered, "Somebody he's cheated will probably shoot him before he gets his hands on it."

"Well, a girl can only wait for the right one for so long. Then she has to look over the competition."

"You can't be serious about Jed. He's a snake."

She stamped her foot. "Now, I don't want to hear any more of this. I know you two had disagreements when you were both children. My brothers fight with their friends every day. But usually, by the next day they forget all about it."

I replied, "If you only knew . . . ."

She jumped in, "He's changed! Why, he's a fine man now, and . . . I think he is going to ask me to marry him."

She looked at me with an expectant look in her eyes. She searched for a certain response, but I didn't know what she wanted. I didn't say anything. Did I see a disappointed look spread over her face? A thought occurred to her, and with a devilish grin she asked me, "Why did you go to church today?"

I felt myself blush again. Suddenly, while looking at her lovely face, I wanted to kiss her. I pulled her closer to me and kissed her lips. She gently pulled away. She reached up on her tiptoes and kissed me back in a way I'd never been kissed before.

Holding her tightly, I could feel her heart racing, and the wonderful smell of her hair intoxicated me. At that moment I wanted to hold her forever. Reluctantly, she pulled away and said, "I've got to get back."

I grabbed her by both hands and, looking into her eyes, said, "Julina, I went to church today because I have been thinking about a lot of things, things about you. I've been struggling with my feelings about the Church. I haven't made my mind up, but my feelings have changed over the last few weeks." I continued, "I need time to work out what I want. If we were to get married, I know you'd want me to go to church. I could never make that promise if I couldn't keep it. Give me a few months."

Julina smiled and said, "I can't wait forever."

I gave her one more lingering kiss, and she rode off. I watched as she disappeared from sight, and with a start I remembered I needed to pick up my sleigh. I jumped onto the stud and took off at a canter to get back to Granite.

Chapter Fifteen

I dropped the steel dust off with Paul and searched for my wagon. I found it in front of the Trout House Saloon. Inside, Rico was speaking with two men I'd frequently seen with Tex.

I spoke to Rico, informing him of my intention to return to Alta. He didn't even look up. I left the saloon, attached the runners to the sleigh, and started up the canyon. What Rico hauled down the canyon in my sleigh puzzled me, but I figured it was better that I didn't know.

A few days later, the story making the rounds in the bars in Alta was that Sheriff Roderick had left town. The woman who cleaned up for him found a note saying he planned to go to Texas on family business. No one raised much fuss because nobody cared for him. But it did seem strange that he should leave so many of his belongings. Nobody saw him leave town. Being that the canyon had only one trail out that time of year, it seemed peculiar. Rumor had it that he left town, but not for Texas. And he didn't leave walking. Typically, no one raised many questions. Within a couple of days, talk turned to other matters and people forgot about Sheriff Roderick.

Over the next several weeks, the days became warmer and the snow melted fast. Every year, during the spring runoff, many of the mines filled with water, making work all but impossible. Several of the biggest mines installed steam pumps, but they hadn't been in operation long enough to tell if they did any good.

Many teamsters couldn't find enough work, so they drifted over to Granite to haul rock to Salt Lake. The pay still wasn't as good, so I stayed in Alta.

I thought about Julina, and since I could never make my letters sound nice, Paul helped me write to her. I even managed to go to church a couple more times. Paul gave me a Book of Mormon; I carried it with me on my wagon and read when I got a chance. Several of the parts were hard for me to understand. Paul was always willing to explain them the best he could.

Weeks passed. A fire in town destroyed several shacks and buildings on Wellington Hill, but other than that, it remained quiet. There hadn't been any shootings, and only a few fistfights had broken out.

One beautiful day a tall, gaunt stranger rode a big red mule into town. He dressed fitting for an undertaker, with a black swallowtail coat and a stove-pipe hat. He had large eyes that bulged and a flat nose. His adam's apple moved up and down his throat like a humming bird inspecting a flower.

Nobody could keep from staring at him as he rode up Walker Street. He tied up in front of Brandy's Restaurant and entered. I heard a voice bellow inside. He confidently strode out, walking across the street to the Grand. With his clumsy walk, he looked all knees and elbows. I heard him say to the group clustered around the bar, "Folks, come outside and witness a miracle." He had this faraway, almost crazy look in his eyes.

I don't think anyone could have refused an invitation like that, so, in stunned silence, the bar emptied. The stranger strode over and climbed the steps to the raised sidewalk in front of the drug store. By this time, thirty curious men had gathered. Word of this strange-looking gent spread like a grass fire, and patrons flooded out from saloons and businesses all along the street. This promise of a miracle had created quite a stir.

The stranger turned, and in a voice like thunder, roared, "I've been sent." A long pause followed and he continued, "I've been sent to perform a miracle in this den of thieves and unholy women."

A murmur ran through the anxious crowd, which was growing as he spoke. With his arms raised like Moses, he looked over the crowd. He seemed to look past his audience rather than at them.

He shouted, "I've a gift. I have a gift! . . . I'd sunk lower than a snake's belly in a wagon rut. There I is in Abilene, lying under the boardwalk with a bottle of corn mash I'd stole while a couple of card sharks were thumpin' each other's heads."

He took a long breath. "I couldn't rub two cents together, and had been drunk so long the months were all blurred together. There, in the muddy street, while I was suckin' on that bottle, walked an angel. Saint Peter hisself walked over and looked under the stoop. I knew he's Saint Peter 'cause he wore them little wings and smoked a white cigar."

The crowd was in awe, holding to his every word.

He rambled on. "Saint Peter tole me to git my scrawny hide out of the mud and find where the devil was workin' overtime. He wanted me to find the towns where heathens had found homes. The kind of places where no saintly person dared walk.

"I've spent the last year visiting such dens of scoundrels. At each town I've used the gift Saint Peter gov me. I brung friends together and got sinners to mend their ways."

The man licked his dry lips. "Since the day I first seen Saint Peter, my lips ain't been near a bottle." He added, almost under his breath, "Ceptin' for holidays and celebratin'."

"I changed my life. Now I've come to Alta to hep you. I hear the anguished souls of all yer friends and relatives wailing to me from that cemetery on the hill, their lives cut short by some murderer's bullet. I've come to bring hope. Reunion for all you and yer dead!" The crowd buzzed with excitement.

"I'll use the gift Saint Peter gov me. I'll bring yer dead back to life!"

I didn't know what to think. The tall, skinny stranger had everyone in the crowd going. His eyes blazed as he spoke.

He spoke softly now. "Some of you're thinking I's crazy. Suckin' on that bottle under that stoop, I'd a thunk it too. But I got religion, and I got somethin' here to show you my power."

He leaned down and opened the small, curious wooden box he'd been carrying. The inside appeared to be filled with straw. He pulled out a ball of striped fur. He held it up, and I could tell that it was a curled-up ground squirrel. He motioned for a young miner standing nearby to come up on the platform. He asked, "Does the pot gut look dead to you?"

The miner looked closely and said, "Dead . . . or sleeping."

The man bellowed, "Tell these sinners, does it feel cold?" The miner touched it and nodded his head.

"This poor animal became the object of abuse by a youngun who had no regard for the saintliness of life. As I watched him, he threw a stone and kilt this poor baby squirrel. With glee the boy—I seen him—tried to take up this squirrel and flee. 'Fore he could git his grubby fingers on it, I put a boot to his behind and sent the imp packing. I placed the poor lifeless body of the squirrel in my box."

He raised the squirrel above his head. "I knew the unbelievin' would need a show. So I brung this here animal."

As he spoke, he rolled the squirrel back and forth in his hands. He possessed a most captivating manner of speaking. People hardly breathed while he spoke. He continued to speak about the tragedy of death and the loneliness of losing a friend or loved one.

Finally, he stopped rolling the squirrel. Holding it tightly against his chest with both hands, he boomed, "Tomorrow night, the night of the full moon, you'll once agin walk and talk with yer dearly departed. Tomorrow night I'll bring the dead back to life!"

He opened his hands and the squirrel peered out. The crowd gasped, and my breath was almost taken away.

Placing the squirrel on a stump nearby, the man continued, "I hope each of you'll consider the needs of the servant who's goin' to deliver the miracle. I've rode myself over many thirsty miles, depriving myself of even a taste of whiskey, all to keep my promise to Saint Peter and bring my gift to you. But I never complained, as hot and dry as it got. I never regretted my promise to not foul my lips with the elixir of the devil, though at times I did get a might thirsty. But I just kept a-ridin', slaving for miserable people like you, bringing such happiness and expecting nothing in return. All I ask is for you to search yer hearts and reach deep in yer pockets. Provide me a meager sum to continue my journey. A small sum'll allow me to continue my mission to the next unholy place I'm called."

He paused and continued softly, "Regardless of whether you feel generous or not, tomorrow yer dead'll walk again!" Then he strode through the crowd, swung onto his long-legged mule, and disappeared up the street.

The squirrel sat on the stump until someone tried to touch it. It scurried down the stump and under the steps. The crowd, electrified by what they saw, retired to the saloon to ponder over a stiff drink. Everyone was stunned and excited about what the stranger had done and said.

Word spread. Before long, every miner and teamster in the valley found himself in one saloon or another, talking about the day's events. Miners quit digging. Teamsters delayed their departures. A mood of great excitement and anticipation swirled through Alta. Most business activities stopped, except whiskey peddling. Everyone waited to greet resurrected friends.

At about seven o'clock that evening, I sensed the mood of the town beginning to change. The owner of the Grand Hotel said sourly, "The hotel's done real well since my partner got shot. He insisted on running it his way, and ran it into the ground. We never made no money when he was alive."

Up and down the street, I found that people were expressing similar views. Those who inherited property wondered if it might make things inconvenient. Several widows and widowers were concerned that the situation might become complicated if their former spouses made an appearance. Tex Hendricks was particularly vocal in not wanting anyone resurrected.

I couldn't keep my eyes open and wandered to my shack, but many stayed up the entire night debating the merits of a general resurrection in Alta.

By the next morning, the excitement had turned to dread. A meeting was held in the Grand Hotel at noon to discuss how to handle this miracle man. The consensus was that the town was better off without a resurrection.

Rico Juarez patted his gun. "A .44 slug will stop him."

"Nah, if he can bring other people back to life, he can sure as hell do it to himself," responded Tex Hendricks.

They argued back and forth until the owner of the Pioneer Store suggested Alta pay him some money to ride out of town. Everyone liked that suggestion. So, upon passing the hat, a couple hundred dollars was raised.

Anticipation filled the air. Everyone waited for the stranger to show up. The afternoon passed, and a few nervous souls threw additional money into the hat in case the total wasn't enough.

At dusk, the mysterious stranger trotted his mule down the silent street. He tied up in front of the Grand Hotel. Tex led the group. "We've had a meeting of town folk and decided that the dead ought to stay put," he said. "Take this here money and jump on yer mule."

The stranger shook his head. He laughed boldly and handed the money back. He turned to the gathering group of people and said loudly, "Friends, I can't disappoint those souls crying to me from their shallow graves. Many of those souls want so badly to be brung back and see you. They must have somethin' important to talk about. In a few moments, I'll loosen the bonds of death."

"Wait right here," Tex menaced.

In a panic, the mob disappeared into the Grand. After loud arguing, everyone felt more money would help change this man's mind. People thrust money from every direction. So much that somebody produced a burlap sack to hold it.

Rico Juarez stood off to the side, spinning the chamber of his pistol. "Let me change his mind," he said in a thick Spanish accent.

Several scampered outside as the miracle man was about to leave for the cemetery. The group confronted him and Tex thrust the sack into his hands. "The town's folk want you to ride away."

One of the shopkeepers piped up, "It would be bad for business if the dead started climbing out of their graves. There'd be too much explaining to do."

"I don't know how I can lower myself and close my ears to the cries of yer dead," the skinny stranger spoke in anguish.

Someone in the crowd rushed up and threw more money into the almost full sack. This caused hysteria as folks pushed and jostled each other to do the same. I got so caught up in the excitement that I almost threw in a twenty-dollar gold piece. While this was going on, the stranger stood back and eyed the sack the way a starved dog looks at a bone. Rico and Tex were eyeing the sack the same way.

The crowd settled down as the stranger got a far-away look in his eyes. He raised both hands to the heavens and pronounced, "It seems that fer the good of this fine town, the dead must be left to rest." He brightened. "I believe it's Saint Peter's will."

The crowd let out a whoop! Someone produced a paper he had drawn that said, "The undersigned will leave the town of Alta and Alta's graveyard intact and let the dead rest in peace."

As the stranger put his "X" on the paper, the crowd let out a cheer. He gave a snaggletoothed grin and handed a stack of gold coins to Rico and another to Tex. "Drinks for all good Christian folk on me," he proclaimed.

The human tide picked up Rico and Tex and rushed them along. I saw Tex, staring wide-eyed at the sack, trying to fight his way free, but the human tide picked him up and swept him into the Alta Brewery, leaving the stranger alone in the street. It took several hours before anyone noticed the stranger had disappeared. Later that night, I saw one of the tavern owners staggering along the street. He had obviously had several drinks. I asked, "How much did we finally give him?"

He stopped and replied, "Must 'a been close to twenty-five hundred dollars, since the sack held more than two thousand when we came out of the hotel the second time." He turned and staggered on.

I found myself standing alone. The thought came to me that nobody had even bothered to ask the stranger his name.

Chapter Sixteen

People in the surrounding communities weren't understanding when they heard that Alta had paid a man twenty-five hundred dollars to not bring their dead back to life. As I rode through Granite, people would stop me and ask if I was in the crowd the day the town gave the man all that money. They'd walk away laughing, shaking their heads.

I'd see them walk to a group, then point at me. Then the whole group would laugh. It got to where I pretended I hadn't heard anything. Those who were away from town and returned after the stranger left couldn't believe the townspeople had been so stupid. A few shop owners finally rode to Salt Lake and tried to get the U.S. Marshall to put together a posse and look for the stranger.

The marshall laughed and said, "What can I do? You're the fools who gave him the money."

It was the talk of the territory until something bigger happened. The Emma stopped hauling ore!

Rumors flew everywhere, but the story whispered by the men working the mine said the vein had run into a fault and disappeared. Needless to say, the Englishmen who paid five million dollars for the mine just two months before were screaming fraud.

Almost a year ago earlier, a Pullman coach filled with English bankers had been part of a train coming from back east. They filled two stage coaches as they made their way up Little Cottonwood Canyon. They wore fancy English wool suits and puffed on large cherrywood pipes.

They inspected the entire mine, saw the ore vein, and inspected the production and shipping records. There were plenty of handshakes and slaps on the back. Then the bankers packed up and set off for England. Nothing was heard for several months, and the local people forgot about the visit. Then, two months ago, the papers announced that the group of English bankers had bought the Emma. The paper said that there had been a bidding war for the mine; several groups wanted to own her. I bet the winners felt like losers now.

The foreman of the Emma, Shaun Doherty, had a few loads remaining. He asked if I'd round up a couple of other teamsters and be at the Emma at first light. Early the next morning, I waited near the fire while the other wagons were loaded.

Shaun had a barrel chest and a thick waist. He couldn't have been more than five and a half feet tall and wore a thick blonde mustache. He spoke with a thick Irish accent and had married one of the prettiest gals in Alta. He worked his miners hard, but he was fair, and everyone liked him.

Shaun was acting different; he seemed agitated. I knew him well enough, having worked almost exclusively for the Emma over the last year. I asked, "What's got you so bothered? Your wife throw you out?"

He smiled. Then, biting his mustache, he said in his Irish accent, "Laddie, let's go inside the tunnel and talk."

We walked a short distance into the mouth, just far enough so we were out of earshot of the teamsters outside. Shaun turned to me and, in a whisper, said, "Laddie, something's been bothering me for some time. I need advice."

From his tone I knew he was serious. I replied, "I'll do what I can, but most people find doing the opposite of what I recommend is usually the best course."

Shaking his head, he explained. "Several months ago, all mining operations in the main tunnel stopped and were shifted to one of the secondary tunnels. This happens from time to time when repairs are needed in the main tunnel."

Pausing, he continued. "Rather than switch back after a couple of days, operations continued in the secondary tunnel for several months. The amount of ore we produced was half of what the main tunnel yielded prior to the switch. A month ago, I received a copy of the shipping records from Sandy Station. It was funny. Those records showed Emma continued to ship as much ore as before."

"Some kind of mistake?"

"Aye, I thought of that," he replied. "I don't think so, laddie. One or two days could be a mistake, but not every day over four months. I figured this to be more than just a mistake."

"What did you do?"

"Made a copy of my production records and spoke to Sheriff Roderick. He seemed interested. Figured the differences were deliberate, too," Shaun said. "When I left the sheriff, he agreed to telegraph the new owners. Same night he disappeared. Thought he might've ridden to Salt Lake, 'cause he didn't trust the nosy telegraph operator. After the note was found speaking of his going to Texas to visit his family, I knew something was wrong."

"How so?" I asked.

"He had no kin in Texas. His only brother lived in San Francisco."

Pushing my hat back on my head, I replied, "So I guess that means the sheriff didn't write the letter about going to Texas."

Shaun looked thoughtful and said, "Aye. I think something happened to him. I think he showed those production and shipping records to someone, and he either ran out of town or got himself shot. I talked to the telegraph operator. He said the sheriff hadn't sent any wires before he disappeared."

"Who else knows about this?" I asked.

"The sheriff told me to be quiet 'til he got some answers,"

Shaun replied. "I hid the production records and waited."

"Where'd you hide them?" I questioned.

He looked at me sternly. "Laddie, I think it's best no one but me knows. They're safe."

"Who else saw the production records?"

Shaun replied, "I always make a copy of production records and send them to the owners. Tex Hendricks works for the owners and takes all my letters to them."

Pondering for a moment, I said, "Then the only people who've had a copy of the figures are you, Sheriff Roderick, and Hendricks, right?" I gulped.

"Aye, laddie, that's right. What's got me bothered is the new owners should see the records, but two weeks ago Hendricks insisted I give him all the copies. I stalled. Two days ago, he and Rico came by to see me. They said if I didn't cooperate I'd regret it."

"What happened?"

"More excuses. Rico threatened to rough me up, until I pulled my little .22 Smith & Wesson out of the pocket of my buffalo skin coat. That changed his tune quick. Hendricks warned that if I didn't cooperate I could expect another visit. Then they left."

"I figured," he continued, "if I gave those production figures to them, I'd be dead by now. As long as I have those figures, they won't kill me because they don't know where I hid them. Once they have those numbers in their hands, they won't want me running around breathing. I'm afraid, laddie, that it would be safer for them if I ceased to be—toes up on Boot Hill, if you catch my drift."

"I guess I'm missing something. What's so important about the production figures that you'd be killed over it?"

He gave me a hopeless look. "Lad, don't you see? Emma produced less ore than she has been given credit for! The vein ran into the fault not one week ago, but about four months ago. Several months before that, the Englishmen paid five million dollars for her."

"A five-million-dollar swindle." I gave a low whistle. "Do the production figures prove what you're saying?"

"Aye, I think it would probably stand up in any court."

"Why don't you just give Hendricks the production figures and disappear?" I questioned.

"I can't do that," he replied. "I have a wife and baby boy. I can't go on the run with them in tow, and I'll never leave them behind. Those Englishmen are on their way here, and it won't be difficult to determine where the ore for the last several months has been coming from. If I disappear it will appear as though I masterminded the scheme. Every lawman and bounty hunter in the territory will be carrying my picture. I'd either find myself in prison for the rest of my life or tied across somebody's saddle."

"You're not painting a promising picture. Can it really be that bad?"

"It's worse," Shaun answered quietly. "Last night I worked inside the mine doing my normal rounds. When I came out, I found where someone had set blasting powder in the side of the opening. The fuse, being wet, went out, or I would have been buried in a cave-in."

His voice dropped to almost a whisper. "Laddie, you're the only one I can trust. These miners here would sell me out for a watered-down drink of sour mash. I'm asking you to take my wife and son to Sandy Station with you tomorrow. But don't let anyone know where you're taking them. I don't dare, since I'm afraid I'll be ambushed if I try."

"What'll you do?"

"The only hope I can see is to try to stay alive until the Englishmen arrive. I've got food stowed in the shack outside the tunnel. I plan on keeping scarce. I'll stay in either the shack or in the tunnel for the next few days. I know those tunnels better than anybody. If someone tries to give me trouble, I can lose myself in there and no one will find me."

"How long can you hide out?" I asked.

"Once the Englishmen arrive, I'll tell them the story, give

them the figures, and hope that Hendricks and his bunch will get nervous and run."

"Have you thought of going to the new sheriff with what you know?"

"Sheriff Florida hasn't been in town long enough for me to make up my mind about him," he said. "For all I know, he works for Hendricks."

"I know Henry Shields, the deputy. He's never worked for those two. When I come back up the canyon, I'll have a talk with him. I'll be by to pick up your wife and son at first dawn tomorrow."

He had a worried look in his eyes. I continued, "Don't worry. Nothing will happen to them."

I heard a boot scuff against rock and turned to see someone jump out of sight around the bend in the tunnel. I took several hurried steps and found myself face to face with Rico Juarez. He stared at me with his flat, expressionless eyes.

How long he had been listening I didn't know. He could have overheard our conversation. Shaun ran angrily toward him and said, "What're you doing sneaking around in this tunnel?"

Rico fumbled for words. "The boss wants you."

"Tell Hendricks," Shaun shouted boldly, "I don't want to see him—and he can go to hell!"

"The boss ain't going to like that," Rico replied with a mean look.

"I don't care what your boss likes. Now get out of here."

Rico's lips tightened as he said, "Hendricks says this is your last chance." He stalked off, never looking back.

I wished Shaun good luck and jumped on my wagon. Early the next morning I left Alta with Shaun's wife, Katie, and their young son. She was short and pretty with her light brown hair. The baby was bald and fat, always wiggling. A beautiful morning greeted us as we bumped down the canyon. I had become accustomed to the jarring wagon ride, but the baby shot his arms out with each bump.

I noticed some large storm clouds in the west. Partway

down the canyon, on the south side, we saw an army of Chinese coolies building the mule tramway to haul ore down the canyon.

The railhead had been installed sooner than most thought possible. During the spring, the railroad had arrived at the mouth of the canyon about a mile southeast of Granite. The loading platform didn't operate yet, so we still traveled to Sandy Station to transport ore, but passengers could leave from the canyon mouth. Buildings in the town of Granite had already started to creep toward the rail terminal. Teamsters in both Granite and Alta knew they'd be out of jobs soon. Some had already begun to drift out of the area, searching for work elsewhere.

Shaun hadn't explained to Katie the full extent of the danger he faced, but he had convinced her to catch the train and visit her parents for a month. She didn't tell me where her parents lived, and I didn't ask. Arriving at the terminal, we found we'd just missed the morning train. Another one wasn't leaving for Sandy until evening. Katie decided she'd rather ride with me than wait.

On the way it began to sprinkle. I pulled the slicker out from underneath the seat. I silently cursed when I saw that it wasn't mine. My slicker had my initials on the back of it, and this slicker did not. I couldn't imagine how it could have gotten mixed up with someone else's.

When we arrived at the Sandy Station, we were early for the train, so I bought Katie dinner while we waited. She told me how worried she felt and that the men who were causing Shaun trouble were dangerous. I paid for the meal while Katie waited outside.

"Taw, you've been so kind to me," she said sadly. "You've brought me all the way here, listened to my worries and carrying on. Thanks for being a friend." She reached up and kissed me on the cheek. I helped her up the step. The worry clearly showed in her face. She knew more about Shaun's troubles than she had let on. "Take care of yourself and that boy," I said. "Try not to worry. Shaun can take care of himself."

She boarded the train and waved. As the train pulled away, she disappeared inside. A sense of dread filled me. Tex and his bunch were killers. I hoped Shaun would be safe. I unloaded my wagon and spent the night at the Railroad Hotel.

Early the next morning I started out for the canyon mouth. All the way there, I couldn't keep from thinking how much Shaun and Katie loved each other. They were really happy. I wanted to have that same relationship with somebody. But not just anybody. I wanted Julina. I'd thought about her constantly since the last time I'd seen her; I knew she must have returned from St. George. I thought again about how Jed had been calling on her, and the thought made my blood boil. At least the letters she wrote showed she hadn't forgotten. After bumping along for an hour, I took the cutoff to Emmaville.

The last few weeks, I'd been reading the Book of Mormon almost every day. I couldn't make up my mind about it. Paul told me the only way I'd be able to make a decision was to pray. I'd thought about it, and a few times I almost tried. But I got all tongue-tied and felt stupid. I didn't know what to say or how to say it. I remembered I'd prayed when I had been caught in the snowslide, but that didn't count because I didn't know I was praying until I was almost finished. As I bumped along in the morning sun, the thought to pray kept coming into my head. I tried to squeeze it out, but it was buzzing around like a fly on a hot August afternoon.

I figured I might as well give it another try, so I stopped the wagon under the shade of some cottonwood trees and climbed down. Willow Creek wound its way through the meadow. The clear water splashed and gurgled between the large boulders. I walked along the creek for a ways until I came to a small, grassy spot shaded by willows and one tall cottonwood.

The meadow was alive with the business of spring. Bees frantically worked the wildflowers. Songbirds squabbled and chased back and forth in the trees. Hungry fish sipped insects fallen from the bank, and high in the sky a redtail hawk wheeled and dove out of sight.

The morning sun had chased the dawn chill from the air. The sky was a brilliant blue, and a few billowy clouds dotted the horizon. New leaves were bursting out on the willows and cottonwoods.

How foolish! What if someone was watching me? I didn't kneel down until I'd looked around. I even took a second look. I felt foolish and walked further along the creek. I knelt and stayed down for the longest time, not knowing what to say or how to say it. Growing up in the Swensen house, I had heard prayers every night, but I would never say one. I didn't know how to put the words together. I was about to get up and walk back, but decided to press on since I'd gotten this far.

I started.

I stuttered and struggled. I found myself blessing the food. That didn't get me anywhere.

I tried to make excuses for why I hadn't prayed in so many years. I didn't feel right doing that, since He already knew the reasons.

Then I found myself blessing every creature ever born. That wasn't what I was here for.

I paused. I remembered what Paul had told me. "Just talk like He's standing next to you. Don't try and be fancy. Just speak how you feel."

I tried. I spoke about my feelings for Julina and even my relationship with Lars. I talked about how sometimes I still missed Ma and about all the worries over the last months. I told Him I made mistakes, but I was trying.

Lastly, I asked about the Book of Mormon.

I wanted to know if it was true. I didn't know what else to say. I got nervous and couldn't remember how to end, so I said, "good-bye." Then I remembered the right way to end and tried that. I know if some churchgoing person had heard my prayer, they would have thought it mighty strange. But I felt better for it.

I climbed back on the wagon and set off for Julina's place. The rest of the ride was peaceful. The birds chattered, the butterflies danced, and the bees buzzed. I was lost in thought.

I found out Julina would be staying in St. George for several more weeks. I left a note and decided to ride to Lars' place. No one was home. A note said Lars had loaded the mob on his wagon and gone to Salt Lake for a few days. I felt overcome, like I needed to get down on my knees and make another try at praying.

I walked into the barn. The smell of hay dust filled the air. The black and white milk cow looked at me, chewing her cud. A tabby cat played with a dangling saddle strap. High in the rafters, a white barn owl dozed.

I climbed to the loft. The old ladder creaked and complained with each step. Rising through the floor, I saw a stack of dusty grain sacks in the corner. Hay was scattered here and there. I kneeled. A warm feeling surrounded me. I repeated the things I'd mentioned in my earlier prayer. I began asking about the Book of Mormon. I felt a warmness from the inside out. It seemed as though someone stood next to me and put his hand on my shoulder.

I knew my prayer had been answered. When I said it aloud, I felt happy and at peace.

I ended my prayer and stayed on my knees, thinking about what I'd felt. All my worries left me. For the first time in my life I felt completely at peace, and I knew what I must do. I wanted to marry Julina. I knew I should keep going to church. I'd have to do some changing. Stop cussing and playing cards. I'd never taken to drinking or smoking. I stood up and threw my chaw out the window and into the corral. I'd never use that again. I'd go to church each week.

I had to do something else. I had to make peace with Lars. But the only way we ever spoke was by yelling. Could I change that much? I didn't know, but I had to try.

I felt ready to take on a grizzly bear and wanted to tell it to the world, but no one was nearby. I couldn't wait to see Julina and tell her what happened. I slept in the loft and left for Alta the next morning.

Chapter Seventeen

After returning to Alta, I put up my team and wandered over to the Grand Hotel. On my way there, I met Sheriff Florida and my friend Henry Shields, the deputy. Florida had become the new sheriff after Sheriff Roderick disappeared. He had recently arrived, so I hadn't met him.

Florida was medium height with black hair and dark brown eyes. He had a narrow face and eyes that were too close together. He also wore a thick handlebar mustache, which he constantly played with.

Paul and I had known Henry Shields as a hunting buddy for years. He was an inch or two taller than Sheriff Florida. He had broad shoulders and a thin waist. His pale blue eyes were set deep in their sockets. His hands were hard and strong from years of felling trees in the canyon. He was an imposing character until a smile could be coaxed from him.

"Howdee," Henry Shields greeted me.

I nodded. Something was up. Neither man was smiling, and Florida scowled.

Florida confronted me. "Stoner, I want to see you in the jailhouse."

Wondering why, I nodded and followed the two men up the steps. Sheriff Florida took a seat behind his desk. He sat thoughtfully and stroked his mustache. I sat on a bench at the side of the desk. Henry walked to the stove, poured a cup of coffee, and took a seat opposite me. Florida, ignoring any pleasantries, began, "How well you know Shaun Doherty?"

It seemed pretty stupid, but I didn't want any trouble. "As well as anybody," I said. "I've hauled for him for over a year. We've talked plenty over that time."

The sheriff furrowed his brow, leaned forward, and asked, "How long have you been seeing Katie Doherty?"

Whoa! That took the wind out of me like a punch in the stomach. I stammered, "What . . . what are you talking about?" Then I got angry. "What the hell gives you the right to ask a question like that?"

The sheriff looked at me with hard, mean eyes. "I have a report that you took Katie Doherty to Sandy Station. Is that true?"

I didn't know what to think, so I sat. The sheriff repeated, "You were seen with Katie Doherty . . . alone."

I exploded. "If Shaun heard what you are saying you'd be looking down the barrel of a colt! Henry, I'm not going to sit and listen to this!" I began to stand.

Glaring, the sheriff threatened, "You're not going anywhere!"

I tried to leave, but the sheriff blocked my path with his leg. Menacingly, he said, "Don't even think about leaving. We found Shaun's body this morning. Right now, we've only got one suspect. And he's standing in front of me."

The sheriff had been holding his gun. He lifted the barrel. "One more step, and that'll be reason enough to blow a hole through Shaun's killer. Sit and answer my questions."

I was too stunned to object. The sheriff sneered, "What do you know about the shooting?"

Turning to Henry, I stammered, "You don't really think I shot Shaun, do you?"

He gave me a hopeless look. The sheriff shouted, "Did you shoot Shaun Doherty?"

"No! Me and Shaun were friends! Why would I shoot him?"

"That's what I want you to tell me!"

Henry Shields jumped in. "Maybe we're getting all bent out of shape over nothing. Shaun was killed late last night or early in the morning. Taw, where'd you spend the night?"

"At Lars' place," I responded.

"Must have been a whole passel of people there, right?"

I answered slowly, "No one. They'd all gone to Salt Lake."

"So nobody can swear knowing where you were all night?" Sheriff Florida asked mockingly.

"No," I shouted, "but some people did see me in Emmaville yesterday, and I passed a couple of teamsters coming up the canyon this morning."

The sheriff passed it off. "You could have ridden to Alta last night, shot Shaun, and left after dark."

"Mighta happened that way," Shields jumped in, "but not likely. More likely, whoever shot him stayed in town. A body riding down the canyon late would be bound to have all the gossips peeking out their windows."

The sheriff grunted. He thought for a moment and said, "I know you took Katie and her baby to the railhead in Sandy. After you arrived in town, you had dinner."

I tried to object, but the sheriff told me to shut up. He continued, "As she was leaving, you kissed."

"Enough!" I bellowed. "You've got your story all twisted up and backwards. I gave her a ride and bought her dinner. As Katie was leaving, she kissed me on the cheek. She was worried about Shaun. She was thanking me for my help, that's all. I've no interest in Katie. I've got me a girl. Everybody who knows me will tell you that."

"I don't believe you. I found this on a shelf in your shack." Florida opened the desk drawer and handed me a small picture in a wooden frame. "Why would you be keeping a picture of Katie in your shack?" the sheriff questioned.

I felt my pulse quicken. My hands got clammy. In desperation, I turned to Henry. "You know this ain't right! I don't know where that picture came from. You know how I feel about Julina!"

Henry shrugged. "Makes no sense to me, but the evidence points to you."

The sheriff, with hate in his eyes, said, "Let me tell you what happened. Katie and Shaun hadn't been getting along. You met, fell in love. She decided to leave Shaun. You gave her a ride to the rail station. That night you came back, hunted up Shaun, and killed him. Don't try and lie your way out of it. We know you did it." His voice sounded triumphant.

"You're nuts. You've been sucking some Chinaman's opium pipe. If I had fallen in love with Katie, I would have gotten on the train and left with her. Why would I come back and shoot Shaun?"

"I wondered that myself, but in looking through your things, I also found this." Florida pulled a bank sack out of a drawer, and from the sack pulled several bank drafts. "These are some of the drafts that were being carried by Lester Sommers before he was robbed and killed a few months back. Looks to me like Shaun knew more about you than you wanted people to know." Florida never took his eyes off me.

"I ain't never seen that bag in my life. Somebody put those things in my shack. Katie can tell you that she loved Shaun. She had no interest in me. Ask her, she'll tell you your story's crazy."

"All right!" Shields had been waiting for something that would help me. "We'll send her a wire and hear her side—see if we got the right story or if we're fishing in the wrong hole. Where'd she go, Taw?"

I felt a sick, sinking feeling in my stomach. "She didn't tell me where she was going, but . . . she said she'd be back in thirty days."

The sheriff glared. "Shaun was murdered last night. You don't have an alibi. His wife left him and you were taking her out of town. We found her picture and some stolen bank drafts in your shack. And now it will be thirty days before we can talk to the only witness that could clear you?"

Florida's voice lowered to a growl. "Shaun was liked by most everyone. I'm not going to let the filthy scum that killed him get away. I'm not going to wait thirty days for testimony while Shaun's killer rides out of the territory."

Henry spoke up, "Taw, this ain't no Sunday picnic we're talking about. The facts the sheriff put together probably wouldn't convict you in front of a judge. But mix a little Valley Tan with those tunnel rats of the Emma, and you could get your neck stretched, with me and the sheriff not being able to stop it." He pointed to the cell block. "Go in there and let's us palaver. Think of something that'll help you."

I walked into the cell block in numbed silence. This couldn't be real. Never in my wildest dreams did I think I'd be in such a fix. My mind raced, and I racked my memory to remember anything.

After what seemed like forever, Henry led me to the office. "The sheriff and I've talked up one side and down the other," he said. "Until we can be sure you is a killer, charging you with the killing of Shaun would be like pulling a trigger. Shaun's got too many friends. Once word got out, you'd be lynched for sure. We're not going to charge you now, but stay in town. If you leave, the sheriff will draw up a warrant for your arrest. We'll have a 'wanted' poster in front of every lawman in the territory. You understand?"

I nodded, then stood and began to gather my things. Several horses thundered to the front door, and men began shouting outside. The sheriff bolted to his feet and hurried outside. I sighed and sat back in my chair. Henry stared toward the wall, never looking at me.

A few moments later, the sheriff walked back into the office and threw something on the desk in front of me. "Recognize this, Stoner?"

I looked at a yellow slicker, my initials visible on the back. "Sure, that's my slicker. It disappeared out of my wagon a while back."

"Do you know where it was found?"

"No, but I'll teach a lesson to the man who had it."

"You won't have to. You already did." The sheriff glanced at

Henry. "This slicker was wrapped around Sheriff Roderick. His body was found in a shallow grave outside of Granite."

With contempt in his voice, the sheriff continued. "You're going to hang for this, Stoner. I want to be the one who kicks the stool from underneath you. You're charged with the killing of Thomas Roderick and Shaun Doherty. You'll be held until a hearing can be arranged."

I couldn't believe my ears. Not me! I tried to pull away, but the barrel of the sheriff's Colt was pointed right at my chest. "Henry," he ordered, "put our prisoner in a cell."

Henry grabbed me by the arm and began walking me back. I gasped, "You can't believe I'm guilty!"

Henry kept walking and whispered, "It don't matter what I think. All that matters is what a jury will think."

He opened the door. I stepped in, and it clanked shut. Looking at me through the bars, he whispered, "I know you didn't do any of this, but you have to admit it looks pretty bad. Sheriff Florida has been given strict orders to clean up this town. I think he's a good man, but if a case can be made and the killer found quick, he'll look like a hero."

He tried to cheer me up. "It's a new jail. There ain't no bedbugs . . . yet."

He locked the door and walked away without looking back. I spent the next several hours trying to figure out how I'd gotten into this mess.

I began to put together the pieces. Someone had stolen my slicker. I remembered having seen it on the trip down the canyon with Tex's ore. Then I remembered thinking something was buried under the load of ore. Could it have been Roderick's body? That would explain why Tex loaded the ore by himself and why Rico unloaded it alone. Could Tex have killed Sheriff Roderick? While I was mulling this over, two horses approached the jailhouse. Peering out, I saw the sheriff and deputy from Granite arriving. Word had already spread that the killer of Shaun and Sheriff Roderick was in jail. I heard groups of men shouting at Sheriff Florida to let them have a look. When that didn't work, men grabbed hold of the bars on the cell windows and pulled themselves up to peer at me. One drunk hung there for several minutes, swearing and spitting at me. I'd finally had enough. When his face was pushed between the bars, I grabbed him by the hair and smashed him in the mouth.

I heard him thud to the ground, and with a string of oaths a bottle smashed against the window bars.

I wondered what Julina would think when she heard I was being held for murder. I hoped I would be able to talk to her, but I wondered if I would ever get the chance. After a long time, I figured there wasn't much sense in worrying because I couldn't do anything anyway. I lay down on the bunk and tried to figure a way out of the mess.

I must have fallen asleep, because I was startled awake when another bottle smashed into the window above my bunk. Bits of shattered glass scattered throughout my cell. Several men were outside shouting and cursing, demanding that the sheriff give me up.

The sun began to sink below the mountains to the west. With it my heart sank. I might not have more than a few hours to live. With a little more whiskey, the mob might get crazy enough to storm the jailhouse. There were simply too many miners in this town for a few underpaid deputies and a sheriff to hold off.

Henry Shields opened the far door and approached my cell. He opened my door and, leaving it open, entered with a stool. Throwing me a dusty hat, pants, and slicker, he said, "Put these on. We're going to try to save your neck. Tex Hendricks is stirring a potload of trouble. He's telling anybody who'll listen that they can't count on a judge to stand up for one of their kind. One way or another, you'll be set free."

"He's started a bloodlust growing," Henry continued. "He's irrigating it with free whiskey. I wouldn't give a penny for your chances if you stay in town tonight."

"Me and the sheriff been thinking hard. This is what we come up with. Just before dark, Florida is going to march

Despane, who'll be dressed like you, over to the old jailhouse. We want to fool the miners into thinking you're being moved. Hopefully, they'll run into the saloons and get the mobs stirred up. We expect them to rush into the street and come after the sheriff. Florida figures to argue as long as he can, then he'll ask that his deputies be allowed to leave the jailhouse. Out will come the sheriff and deputy. Once they are safely away, the mobbers will be turned loose on an empty jailhouse.

"While all of this is happening, you and me are going to ride down the canyon. Those miners are going to be madder than a bunch of wet hens. With luck, the two of us will be several miles down the canyon by the time the mob figures out what's happened. Now here, get into Despane's duds."

"Do you really think this'll work?" I asked.

"Might. But if we don't try something, you're as good as dead."

"What if we're stopped by someone who knows me?"

Shields answered, "You'd better hope that churching you been doing lately done some good. Got to make you look real. Carry Despane's weapons, no bullets. If we get stopped, use your spurs and hope they ain't holding steady. My gun ain't going to keep a mob from firing.

"Taw," he went on, "this gives you some kind of a chance. Better than sitting waiting 'til they come and get ya. Now, you ready to go?"

"Sure," I said hopelessly. We left the cell chamber and entered Sheriff Florida's office. Despane was easily recognizable. He always wore a large, soft-brimmed hat, and he carried an old Kentucky long rifle. It took a minute for Despane to put on my clothes.

I had to admire Despane. He could get shot in the back by someone waiting in the street, but he was willing to take this chance so I'd get to a trial. In his position, I hoped I'd do the same.

With Sheriff Florida and the deputy holding rifles at the back of the handcuffed Despane, the three walked quickly up the street. Just like we hoped, several men ran into the saloons.

At the same time, the two of us walked out and mounted the waiting horses. We started up the street in the opposite direction at a brisk walk. We couldn't move too fast lest we attract attention.

Shields looked back and noticed that the three men were entering the old jailhouse at the same time the first group of drunken miners poured into the street. We were leaving the built-up part of Walker Street when out of the willows at the side of the road a group of armed men stopped us. I felt my breath rush out, and my palms got sweaty.

A booming voice challenged us. I recognized it as Tex Hendricks. "You wait right there. We're not letting Shaun's killer get out of here alive."

My heart sank. Could Tex have recognized me? By now it was so dark I couldn't make out any of the men's faces. I could just see silhouettes.

Shields shouted back, "You're interfering with the law. Sheriff Despane and me got business in Granite." With that, Shields cocked his Winchester and pointed it at of Tex's chest. "We ain't going to let any mob run this town tonight."

Tex sneered, "You wouldn't dare shoot a man who wasn't holding a gun."

Shields chuckled, "Don't bet your life! Half the people in this town would let out a cheer if my gun happened to fire. If any of your friends here raises an eyebrow, my trigger finger just might get excited."

I don't know if Henry was bluffing or not, but the mob bought it. None seemed eager to challenge his loaded Winchester. In the distance, from the direction of the old jailhouse, we heard the crack of a rifle. A man's voice bellowed above the din, "We got him cornered."

Several more shots rang out. It sounded like some of the men in the sheriff's group might have fired in return. The mob confronting us lost interest trying to figure out what was going on. I saw a chance, gave my horse a slap, and pushed my way through. Henry, doing the same, cleared the crowd, and together we began to canter down the wagon road. I peeked over my shoulder, but couldn't make out anyone following us. Our ruse had worked.

We picked up the pace, trying to put as much distance between us and Alta as possible before complete darkness settled in. We kept up the pace all the way down the canyon. Hooves thundered over the rocky road, and froths of foam formed on the horses' necks.

Nearing Granite, we slowed to a canter, and for the first time I told Henry about what Shaun had told me. I told him about why I took Katie Doherty to Sandy Station, and about Tex's role in the whole scheme. I also told Henry what Shaun thought about the swindle of the new owners of the Emma. I next told him about the ride down the canyon with Rico and my suspicion that something was buried under the load of ore. I now figured it must have been the sheriff's body. Shields pulled down his hat and didn't say a word. When we reached the corrals at Granite, he spoke up. "Taw, if what you're saying is true, these men ain't going to let you live to stand trial. Tex and Rico are dry-gulchers. If they figure Shaun told you all he knows, they'll find a way to kill you—unless you can find a way to get them in jail first."

He continued, "I haven't told you everything the sheriff knows. It was Tex who talked the sheriff into snooping in your shack after we found Shaun's body."

I blurted out, "You don't think I . . . ."

"Of course not. I know Katie, and I know how she felt about Shaun. Looks like Tex has gone to considerable trouble to build a case against you. Probably some scheme to tie Shaun to the swindle. Lay the blame on someone else so he can get away clean."

Henry swallowed and continued, "Tex has made it pretty easy for Sheriff Florida. The sheriff is under considerable pressure to put an end to the killings. As long as a reasonable case can be made and somebody's in jail, Florida will look like he's doing his job. He ain't as concerned about getting the guilty man as he is about looking like a hero to the judge.

"Florida ain't been in Alta long. He still goes by all the rumors. He figures anybody who lives here must have killed somebody sometime. The way he sees it, anyone who gets hanged, whether guilty or not, is one less criminal running the streets."

I asked, "What're you saying?"

Henry replied, "Once I get you to Salt Lake, the sheriff ain't going to want the case against you to fall apart. No matter what other evidence I can turn up, he isn't going to make any effort to clear you. Once the town quiets down, Tex will be able to talk him into bringing you back to Alta. On the trip back up the canyon, I imagine someone will dry-gulch you from the cliffs."

"Henry, what am I going to do?"

He pondered for a moment. "Taw," he said, "can you get a fresh horse and change of clothes from your brother Paul?"

"Yeah. Rather than make the ride back to Emmaville every night, he usually spends the night in the tent with the cooking supplies. He'll have some spare clothes."

"Hurry, change and get that horse. I've got an idea."

Chapter Eighteen

Paul wasn't in, so I left him a note. I threw a saddle on the steel dust stud, changed my clothes, picked up a bedroll, and hurried back to the road. A clear starlit sky greeted me, and a cool wind made the steel dust frisky. A sliver of moon gave just enough light to travel.

As we rode, I thought about everything that had happened in the last twenty-four hours. I had decided I wanted to marry Julina, and for the first time I'd prayed and knew somebody was listening.

The bitterness that had lingered with me since the death of Ma was gone. Sure I missed her, but I knew that I could see her again someday. That made me feel good.

I needed to ask Lars to forgive me. I'd caused him so much trouble and had been hard to get along with. He'd tried to be a friend and a pa to me. He'd tried to show me he cared, but I never let him get close. That was going to change.

How was it, when I'd made such changes and things seemed to be going right, that I could get involved in such a mess? Try as I might, I couldn't come up with a way to clear myself. I was going to have to rely on Henry Shields to keep me out of the cemetery at Collins Gulch.

We rode, always keeping near the hillside. We veered off the wagon road after we passed Emmaville. When we reached a point where we could see the lighted windows of McGee's Tavern, we reined in.

Henry spoke. "The only way to give you a chance is for you to make an escape. Then you're going to have to make a decision. You can run and take your chances. If you can make it to Canada or Mexico, after ten years or so you could probably come back. Or you can try to clear yourself. When Katie comes back, I figure we can clear you of Shaun's killing. Sheriff Roderick is another matter. We're going to have to capture and question Tex or Rico.

"But Sheriff Florida is not going to try to bring in either one," he went on. "They're too good with their guns. I can't help you either, Taw. It would be suicide for me to try to bring in any of Tex's bunch alone. If you want a clean slate, you're going to be pretty much on your own. You'll have to catch one of them, then go to Salt Lake and let the judge hear your story.

"If word gets out that I let you go, I might swing. You hit me over the head and escaped. I have to trust you to never say anything different."

Looking him in the eye, I answered, "You don't need to worry."

He gave me his Colt and his Winchester; he kept the Kentucky rifle and told me he expected the guns back, and that I'd better take care of them. When the next cloud passed in front of the moon, I jumped onto the steel dust stud and galloped up the canyon. I figured it was safest for me to put some miles between me and the law. Then a thought struck me: rather than spend the night in the canyon, why not take Scott's Pass out? There was endless open country on top. I could lose myself for weeks.

The climb had been steep and exhausting, and when I finally reached the summit, the sky was just beginning to gray. I hitched the steel dust at the first level spot with a few trees, rolled out my bedroll, and immediately fell asleep.

I was awakened well past daylight by a scolding jay. I rode down to a small spring in a thick grove of chokecherries and built a small fire, where I warmed water for coffee and tried to figure a plan.

I decided the best idea was to keep moving in case someone tried to find me. After a few weeks, I'd sneak into Granite and talk to Paul. I hoped Henry would have some news. In the meantime, I'd spend the next week playing Injun, hunting and fishing.

The steel dust stud quietly cropped the lush, high mountain grass. The meadow, alive with fluttering butterflies and honeybees, was sprinkled with bell flowers and columbines. I mounted and wandered to the northeast. I hoped to make a large loop around both Big and Little Cottonwood Canyons, approaching Granite from the south. Riding through the deep grass and scattered stands of pine, I noticed a north-facing slope that had burned at some time in the last few years. A few lone, charred stags dotted the hillside. Where the trees had been, berry bushes now grew. Taking off my hat, I gorged myself on juicy ripe berries.

But I was not the only one with an eye for berries. Fresh bear signs marked another crossing. A redtail lazily circled above my head. Its young followed, shrieking for food, but the adult did its best to ignore the pesky youngsters. The hawks spiraled and disappeared behind a ridgeline to the south.

I thought back. As a young boy, I'd always taken time to hike into the mountains with my gun, doing exactly what I was doing now, sitting and watching the world around me. Every day I had found new adventures, and had loved everything—the sights, smells, and tastes—about the high mountains. But, like many of the men in any mining town, a lust for money had turned my head.

I gave my horse his head over the next two days. I hunted, fished, and thought about Julina. I thought about my prayer in Lars' barn. For the first time in my life, I somewhat understood why Lars, Paul, and Lucy had always been so devoted to their church. Rather than look for the good in churchgoing people, I'd been quick to criticize. I had focused on little points of hypocrisy, yet I was blind to the same faults in myself and others.

Late in the afternoon of the third day, a heavy rain began to fall. I'd not traveled far that day, so I decided to return and camp in the spot where I'd spent the previous night. It had been a good campsite. A rock overhang would protect me from the rain, and tall, dense pines offered me a supply of dry wood.

It was dusk when I reached the campsite. I jumped from my horse and began to look for dry tinder. I was a fool for not noticing sooner, but there in the ground was a boot print, smaller than my own, with the mark of three large rowls behind the heel. Only a Mexican spur left that mark. My stomach wound itself into a knot as I remembered the only man in these parts who wore Mexican spurs: Rico Juarez!

The rain began to fall in a heavy mist, thunder boomed off the nearby ridge tops, and lightning danced between the peaks. Kneeling, I examined the track. It had been made earlier, at least several hours ago, but how much longer I couldn't tell. For all I knew, Rico could be looking at me through the sights of his rifle right now. Pulling the Winchester from its boot, I grabbed the reins of the steel dust and ran at an angle toward the ridge top. If Rico was holed up nearby, I'd rather be above him than have him shooting down.

Nearing the crest, I mounted my horse and ran him through the open meadow lying between me and the ridge top. With each crack of thunder, the young horse bucked and pulled on the reins. The air was cold, but sweat trickled down my neck. Nearing the ridgeline, I saw a flash of lightning illuminate the entire hillside. I heard a crack like a harsh snap of thunder. My left arm was suddenly knocked across the front of my body. Almost at the same moment, another white-hot piece of metal sliced across my ribs like a sharp knife. The stud bolted, and I instinctively grabbed a handful of mane and held on.

Upon reaching the top of the ridge, the steel dust sprinted

along the ridge rather than down the other side. I held my useless left arm tightly to my side, a burning pain shooting through my ribs with every lunge. The rifle cracked again. The steel dust veered sharply right. Looking up, I saw that we were heading for a narrow gap between two trees, and my left leg and shoulder smashed into the first of them. I dropped and skidded along the muddy ground.

I found myself lying in a heap, gasping for air. I'd been dazed, but I forced myself to my feet and staggered into the cover of a grove of aspens. I didn't know how badly I'd been hit, but I could still move. After dumping me, the mustang had disappeared down the slope. Somehow, I'd held onto my rifle. I wasn't sure where Rico was, but I knew he would be hunting me. I crept carefully down the ridge opposite where I'd camped, then traveled further down and turned across the hillside. A horse nickered from a cluster of short pines to my left. Dropping on my stomach, I crawled through the freezing mud toward the sound. Two could play this hunting game.

Peering from behind a small bush, I saw the outline of two horses, their ears pricked, looking in my direction. I looked again and counted two horses and five pairs of legs! Sarah hadn't sent me to school for nothing. Even as bad as I was at figures, I knew that somebody was standing between those horses. I thought about sneaking off. Wounded as I was, I wasn't going far before two men on horseback could catch me. My only hope was to even the stakes.

I couldn't get a clear shot at the man between the horses, and I didn't know where his partner was hiding. My left arm wasn't good for anything, so I rested the barrel of my gun on a rock. I didn't like the thought of it, but if I was going to escape I had to put Rico and his partner on foot. At the next flash of lightning, I fired two quick shots, one at the head of each horse. They dropped stone dead, and the man, caught by surprise, stood in the open for just a moment. As he dove for cover, I snapped off a hasty shot. I heard him yelp. Then the sky went black.

I turned and wound my way through the timber in the opposite direction from the ridgeline. The two men following me probably wouldn't continue on foot. They might spend tomorrow trying to find the steel dust, but that young mustang would be forty miles away by morning.

I took cover under tall pines, and finding shelter from the rain, tried to more closely examine my wounds. The first bullet had struck my left forearm and passed completely through. The second entered the skin on my left breast and lodged outside my ribs, under my skin. I could feel the slug under my skin near my armpit. I tore up my scarf and used it as a bandage to stop the bleeding.

My ribs hurt every time I breathed. I wanted to stay right where I was, but I had to get as far from Rico as I could. Earlier in the day, I'd seen an Indian camp a couple of miles off in the direction I was heading. I hadn't heard of any renegades in these parts, so I hoped they'd be friendly. Rico wouldn't follow me into an Indian camp.

I walked for what felt like an eternity. The rain had stopped, and stars had begun to peek out between the clouds. At first I attempted to conceal my tracks, but the loss of blood began to cloud my judgment. I became clumsy. My steps wandered from a straight line. I feared I'd begin to walk in a circle, so I sighted a star, and keeping my eyes on it, stumbled on. I found myself shivering and wanting to lie down and sleep. After a while, all my mind could focus on was one step, then another. I walked like a man going to his grave: a step, a pause, another step, and a stumble. My shivering became so severe that my head nodded, and somewhere the rifle slipped from my grasp. How long I walked I have no idea. Several times I slipped. It took all my effort to force myself to my feet and continue on. I refused to rest, because I was certain I would never get up. Vaguely, I thought I heard barking. I thought I saw the outlines of several tepees. I had to keep walking. Stumbling, I fell in the mud, and a dog snarled. Then everything went black.

Chapter Nineteen

As if in a fog, I heard women talking nearby. It took a moment for me to realize that I couldn't understand what they were saying. I wanted to open my eyes further, but it was too easy to lie there with them closed. I stirred again. My nose was greeted with a putrid smell. My mouth tasted like something had died inside it. I hurt everywhere and wanted to throw up. I felt terribly thirsty. My stomach seemed to be on fire.

As my senses cleared, I found myself under a bearskin inside of a tepee. An Indian woman and a girl were sitting in the dirt at the entrance. They heard me stir. She motioned to the young girl, who disappeared outside and returned with a buffalo horn. It was filled with some dark liquid.

She brought the horn to my mouth, and the smell almost made me lose my last meal. I pushed it back, but she was insistent and held it to my lips. I held my nose and took a sip. I couldn't believe it. It tasted worse than it smelled.

I tried to turn my head and push it away, but I finally tired of fighting and took a few more sips. I felt as though I'd been branded on the inside.

I moved. My wounds had been bandaged. I tried to stand, but my side felt like the wounds were tearing open. In a cold sweat, I sat back down.

An older brave wearing a loincloth and moccasins entered the tepee. I'd known him years before when he traded with Lars. Lars had called him Broken Nose. The line of his nose twisted down his face like a snake. He was the leader of the band of Shoshone who spent most of the summer camped up the Little Cottonwood. Lars had been fair to him and his people. I was glad now. From his eyes, I could tell he remembered me.

He grunted. The two women disappeared, and he sat down across from me. He told me how I had staggered into camp. Several of his braves had found me and brought me to his tepee. I'd become hot with a fever and had slept four days. A medicine man bandaged me and sang over me. He told me that made the fever go away.

He also told me his braves had backtrailed me and found the two horses I'd shot. They also found that I'd shot a man. I'd not wounded him seriously, since he and another man had hiked back into Big Cottonwood Canyon. I asked him how he knew. He said the story was told in the signs on the ground. He handed me my rifle and I thanked him again. He just grunted and abruptly stood and walked outside.

Over the next few days, I gained strength. But I couldn't sleep because of the terrible itching. Looking at my arms, I discovered my skin was covered with red welts, and I realized the skins I'd lain in were infested with lice. It pained me to rise, but I moved outside as quickly as I could.

In the high mountains, the sunny days were warm, but the nights felt like early spring. The warm days triggered an explosion in all kinds of critters that tormented a fellow. I discovered that most of the Indians slept outside and hung their skins during the day. They preferred chilly air to the biting bedbugs.

In three weeks, I had gained enough strength to get around. My arm had healed, but my chest still bothered me. I may have broken some ribs that were slow to heal. I spent hours every day thinking about Julina, how much I missed her, what she must be thinking. If only I could talk to her or get a letter to her.

Time passed slowly with little to do. The Indian women and

children spent their days collecting berries that were abundant. The men spent most of their time doing nothing. Occasionally they made arrows or chipped arrowheads. Some of the braves went hunting, but little effort was put into the task. They were preparing for the fall buffalo hunt.

There wasn't much I could do. One arm had a hole in it, and I couldn't lift my other arm because of my sore ribs. When I recovered to the point where I felt I could ride a horse and shoot a gun, I talked the chief into giving me a ride down the ridge to Granite.

He let me off a mile up the hill. I decided to wait for dark then sneak down to Paul's tent. I thanked him and his people for all their help, and he rode off.

I waited on the hillside all afternoon. As dusk approached, I started down. I found Paul's tent; he wasn't there, but I rifled through all his belongings looking for food. After three weeks of eating ill-tasting Shoshone fare, I was eager for anything that tasted good. I found a small pouch of jerky and some chocolate I knew he'd been saving—but that only stopped me for a moment. Paul entered the tent just as I licked the last of his chocolate from my guilty fingers. He looked at me with his hands on his hips and said, "You know, Taw, you're more trouble than you're worth. Just when I'm convinced you're dead, you pop up again!"

He strode to me and threw his arms around me. Then he picked up a paper that had been sitting on a table in the corner and said, "Here. Read about yourself."

I picked up the Alta paper and read, "Taw Stoner wanted in connection with the shooting of Shaun Doherty and former Sheriff Roderick, escaped from Deputy Henry Shields at Silver Fork." The paper talked about my supposed romance with Katie Doherty, and then expressed the outrage of the town of Alta over my escape. According to the report, Deputy Shields had been taking me to Salt Lake when I'd wrestled away his gun and escaped. The paper also said that Deputy Shields, fearing to face the outraged citizens of Alta, had not returned to town.

I looked up when I finished, and Paul spoke to me. "You always told me you were going to be famous. I guess one way is as good as another."

"You don't think I murdered those men, do you?"

With an amused look he said, "Almost, but I talked to Henry, and he told me the story you told him. Somebody wired Katie, and she returned and spoke to the sheriff. Sheriff Florida gave up trying to convict you of Shaun's murder, but he still feels he has a case against you for killing Sheriff Roderick, and he's doing everything he can to find you."

"The reason I didn't go into the hills looking for you after I got the steel dust stud back was that the sheriff watched me closely. The steel dust wandered into Silver Fork, and somebody recognized my brand. When I picked him up, I saw the blood on the saddle and expected the worst. I told Shields about it, and he feared Rico had dry-gulched you. With you gone so long, I'd about given up. I was going to claim your things for my own."

"Great," I said, "to know you were so worried about my wagon and gear."

"But," Paul continued, "my big brother always seems to find a way to do what I don't expect."

"What's happened with Shields?"

Paul replied, "He stayed out of Alta for a spell, but recently returned. He tried to convince Florida of your innocence, but the Alta sheriff won't make a move against Tex or his men.

"Since the Emma closed, miners have been leaving like rats jumping ship. Most are going to Park City or Tintic to find work. The rail line has started shipping ore from the mouth of the canyon. They named the new ore station Wasatch. It put most of the teamsters out of work. When the mule tram is finished this fall, all the remaining teamsters in Alta will be out of jobs. Even some of the men who'd worked for Tex left town. Several rode out yesterday. Shields hopes that Sheriff Florida may find new courage once a few more of Tex's hired thugs leave.

"Shields told me he wanted to talk with you if you ever

came back. Wait in my tent while I ride and get him."

He was pulling on his boots when I asked, "Do you know anything about Julina?"

He looked down at his boots. "Sarah's been talking to one of Orson Smith's wives. She says when Orson read about you in the papers, he went into a tirade about how you were no good. Julina was crushed when she read about Katie Doherty. She'd turned down a proposal from Jed Mathews, but I heard that at the encouragement of her father, she's seeing him again."

My face got hot as he continued, "When Katie returned to town and disputed the story of her romance with you, the papers didn't carry it. In fact, there's been no mention in the papers that you are no longer wanted in connection with Shaun's murder. I only found out about it through Henry yesterday."

"What's happened with Julina?"

"Jed showed up yesterday. I don't know what's happened, but I know her father's put her under considerable pressure to marry him."

"I have to see her right away," I said.

"Too risky," Paul warned. "Sheriff Florida has been watching both my tent and Julina's house. You got in here all right, but you'll be pushing your luck if you go there."

"Then help me, Paul. If I write her a note, will you get it to her?"

He gave me a grin and said, "Sure."

He left, and I was as jumpy as water on a hot griddle. I tried to sleep. After an eternity, a horse galloped to a stop outside and Paul ducked inside. He thrust a folded paper into my hands and I read:

Taw,

The owners of the Emma arrived in Alta earlier this week. They looked over all the records kept by Tex Hendricks. What they saw wasn't the same as what Shaun told you. I suspect Tex doctored the numbers. There are several questions raised, but no fraud can be proved. One of Tex's men rode into town with a minor gunshot wound. Rumor has it that you fired on him. Another rumor is that

Tex is offering five hundred dollars to the first man who kills you or brings proof that you're dead.

I don't know what to think about Florida. The only evidence he possesses linking you to the murder of Sheriff Roderick is the word of Tex that he found your slicker wrapped around the sheriff's body. Yet he's not about to let go of the idea that you killed Roderick. He aims to see you hang. Seems like he's either being paid by Tex or been scared into ignoring him.

I trust you'll burn this letter. I'll have to be careful leaving town, since Tex is having the roads watched.

Henry

P.S. I heard Rico is coming down the canyon tomorrow with supplies for Silver Fork. If you can find a way to get ahold of him and take him to the judge, you might get the truth. Good Luck.

I gave the letter to Paul. He read it and asked, "What are you going to do?"

"I don't know yet, but I'm not going to spend the rest of my life running. I'm gonna capture Rico and take him to Salt Lake."

Paul said, "You don't think you're going to do it alone, do you?"

I smiled. During the next hour, we figured a plan to get Rico to Salt Lake.

It was too risky for me to stay in Paul's tent any longer, so he borrowed a buckboard. When no one was looking, I crawled under the canvas he piled in back. We started on the road toward Emmaville. Once Paul left the canyon mouth, he found a secluded spot where I climbed out and hid in the heavy brush that lined the road. Paul continued on to deliver my letter to Julina.

As I crawled up the steep hillside, buck brush tore at my skin. Sweat stung the wounds and dripped into my eyes. I waited under the branches of a pine. Paul had given me water and food, and I'd brought several newspapers from his tent. I wanted to catch up on the doings about town. I tried to doze, but the horse flies almost ate me alive, so I gave up and spent my time swatting the pests. After killing over thirty, I considered myself quite a hero.

From where I climbed, I could see Emmaville to the north. Up the canyon and to the east, I saw Wasatch Station. I had only been gone a month, and I could see changes. It seemed that most of the buildings in Emmaville and Granite City had moved to the new town of Wasatch. Sooner or later, I guessed, both towns would be abandoned or moved. I hadn't asked Paul what Lars planned to do now that the railroad would be hauling granite to Salt Lake.

I kept thinking of Julina. I wanted more than anything to see her, to hold her. Yet I feared that now I'd lost her. There was still a chance she'd listen when I saw her again, but the thought didn't give me much hope. I wondered if my problems were the kind I should pray about.

I thought of her seeing Jed. That made me cussing mad. I picked up the newspapers tried to get my mind off her and Jed.

One article made me chuckle. It read, "No News—There is no news whatsoever stirring in Alta, and under the circumstances, we find it difficult to fill up two or three columns with local matter. If some kind individual would start a controversy or get up an excitement of any kind, it would be a great relief to us."

I sure could have traded places with that editor. I'd had far more excitement than I cared for. I lay back and thought—soon Julina would be reading my letter. Would everything be all right?

At dusk I met Paul. The steel dust stud was tied behind the wagon. He reined in with a sick look on his face. "She wouldn't take your letter."

I was shocked, since this was totally unexpected. He said, "She told me to tell you to stay with Katie Doherty. I tried to explain, but Jed closed the door in my face."

He handed me back the letter, and I dropped it in the dust. My life was coming apart. The law wanted me in jail, Tex wanted me dead, and my girl didn't care anymore.

Chapter Twenty

I rode the steel dust up into the mountains, made a dry camp, and spent most of the night thinking.

The next morning found me high on the mountainside above Granite. The chill in the mountain air refreshed me. I sat on a large rock, soaking up the warming rays of the morning sun. The plan I had worked out with Paul was simple. He'd wait in Granite for Rico to come down the canyon. After Rico passed, he'd follow in his buckboard with a red blanket in the back.

Once he passed Emmaville, I'd ride ahead and wait. When he came into view, I'd get the drop on him. Paul would be nearby in case I needed help.

I'd tie him up and hide him under the blanket in Paul's buckboard. Then I'd ride to Salt Lake. Paul would take the steel dust and let Henry know. We'd meet in Salt Lake at the judge's. If Rico talked, I went free. If he didn't talk, I went to jail. I hoped when Henry arrived, Rico would be charged with the murder. There were some holes in my plan, but I didn't have any other options.

I camped so high up, the people working at the granite quarry looked like ants. After several hours, I noticed a wagon heading toward Emmaville. Behind it was a wagon with a red blanket.

I hid in scrub oak above Emmaville and waited. Rico's wagon came into view. He rode alone, passing directly through town and continuing toward the cutoff to Silver Fork. Putting spurs to the steel dust, I rode to head him off. After some rough riding, I picked my way up a small rocky draw that intercepted the road. I picketed the stud a distance from the road, so he wouldn't scent the coming horses. If he did, he'd nicker and alert Rico that a rider was near.

I crawled behind a small stony outcropping and waited. As I waited in the hot sun, sweat began to trickle down my face. I tried to change position, but there was no shade anywhere. The heat became unbearable, and I was about to move when I heard the creak of the wagon and the chopping of horse's hooves.

Looking carefully, I still couldn't see anything. A small rise blocked my view—but a cloud of powdery dust was hanging in the air beyond the rise. The wagon approached at a slow, steady pace. A horse blew and nodded into view. I ducked my head and listened.

As his horses came abreast of me, their ears shot up and they turned their heads toward me. I jumped out, leveling the Winchester, and shouted, "Rico! Drop those reins!"

My sudden appearance startled him, but he recovered quickly, and I saw by his eyes that he would not make this easy. I shouted, "Drop 'em. Now! I'm already wanted for a murder I didn't commit—another won't make any difference."

He relaxed his grip, and I motioned him off the wagon. I saw he wasn't wearing a gun, but I knew he'd have one within easy reach. I walked him away from the wagon and waited for Paul to catch up. Paul drew abreast and jumped to the ground, gun in hand. He walked to the back of Rico's wagon. With a laugh he remarked, "You'll never guess what's back here—coffins."

"What're those for?" I asked.

Rico replied, "Not enough men dying lately in Alta, so the undertaker sold them to a man in Silver Fork."

I had an idea. "Paul, hold your gun on him while we load one of these coffins in your buckboard."

With Rico's reluctant help, we hefted one of the coffins onto the buckboard. Rico climbed on and pulled while I stayed on the ground and pushed. Then Paul took Rico's wagon and hid it in heavy brush. I told Paul where his horse waited, and he went for it. Meanwhile, I motioned for Rico to get into the coffin.

"What!" he exclaimed and cursed at me.

"You heard me. If you don't move quick, I just might figure it's too much trouble to take you back alive." I pointed the rifle at the open coffin. He stared at me defiantly.

To show I meant business, I cocked the rifle and took a couple of steps toward him. He stood on the buckboard and slowly lay down inside. I nailed on the lid over his vehement cursing. Then I tied the coffin down. I told Paul to meet me in Salt Lake as soon as he could find Henry Shields.

I slapped the horses and set off, moving at a fast pace all the way to Salt Lake. The coffin bounced all over the back of the buckboard. Whenever I went over a large bump it would jump several inches, smashing back onto the bed of the wagon, and I'd hear a gasping moan from Rico. I got a kick out of it.

Several hours later I arrived in Salt Lake, where I trotted to the stable and gave the hand a dollar to rub down and feed the horses. Using my knife, I cut the ropes and pulled the nails out of the coffin. Rico staggered out, tame as a newborn puppy.

I told him we were going to see the judge, and he'd better cooperate and talk or me and my friends might have to put that coffin to a better use. With my gun pointed at his back, we walked over to the courthouse.

A federal marshal met us. He said I wasn't going a step further with a loaded gun. I told him my story. He thought for a moment and told me that Rico wasn't going anywhere until he got to the bottom of what had happened. He also said I'd have a chance to tell my story to the judge, if I handed over my gun.

I had no guarantees that anyone would believe me, or that

anything could be proved. Yesterday, I had talked to Paul about this in his tent. He told me as long as I tried to do the right thing, I'd have to have faith that everything would work out. It's a lot easier to talk about giving up my weapons than to actually do it.

I gave the marshal my gun and he walked me to a cell. Rico was directly across from me. I lay down, and it felt good. I closed my eyes and drifted off to sleep.

Chapter Twenty-One

Rattling on the bars in my cell woke me up. Through the bars I saw Paul and Henry Shields peering at me. Shields asked the deputy to open Rico's cell. They marched Rico down the corridor to an adjoining room. Paul and I talked for a while until Deputy Shields returned a smug-looking Rico to his cell. Then Shields opened my cell, and I followed him down the corridor.

I took a seat while the judge stepped in and sat down. Shields looked at me and said, "We spoke to Rico, but he wouldn't talk. We asked him about Sheriff Roderick's body. He said he was riding with Tex and saw something partially covered. He climbed off his horse and kicked away some loose dirt. Under the dirt, draped in your slicker, he found Roderick. That's all he'd say."

I replied, "That surely can't be enough to hold me."

The judge said, "If that is all Sheriff Florida has on you, I'll set you free. But he issued a warrant for you, so I must assume he has more than Rico's testimony."

"What does that mean?"

The judge replied, "I'll telegraph Sheriff Florida and ask him to show me the evidence he has."

"What about the information I have?"

"Deputy Shields told me some of your story, and I am interested in hearing what you have to say."

I told him about the wagon trip down the canyon with Tex's ore. I talked about the conversation with Shaun Doherty and the production figures he'd hidden. I told him why I took Katie Doherty to Sandy Station. Finally, I told him about the ambush in the hills above Big Cottonwood Canyon, and how I feared that if Florida took me back to Alta, I'd be killed.

The judge listened to everything, asked me several questions, and told me he would get in contact with the English company that had purchased the Emma. "You tell an interesting story," he said. "The Salt Lake newspapers reported this morning that the newspapers in England are screaming about the fraud perpetrated by the sale of the Emma. They're demanding that the United States Government force the reversal of the sale. If the sale is not reversed, the English newspapers are calling for England to declare war with the United States."

"You must be kidding."

"I wish I was," he replied. "You've put yourself in the middle of one of the biggest scandals to hit these parts. I'm certain many people are going to want to hear your story first-hand. I am going to hold you in jail for two reasons. First, because I want to see all of Sheriff Florida's evidence, and second, if your story is true and I let you out of jail, you might have a bullet in your back by nightfall."

He excused himself and the deputy escorted me back to my cell. I sat in the cell for several days waiting for Sheriff Florida to arrive. Rico, who sat across the hall in his cell, never looked at me and never said a word. The marshal questioned him several times, but he didn't scare and he wouldn't confess.

In the meantime, I stared at the walls. I wrote another letter to Julina and asked Paul to deliver it when he returned to Granite. I hadn't heard anything, so I didn't know if she had accepted it.

Not knowing what she thought drove me crazy. I couldn't

keep my mind off thoughts of her with Jed walking hand in hand, or thoughts of her believing I loved someone else when she was the only person I wanted. Jed would be poisoning her against me. There was no way for me to tell her the truth. I just hoped she'd give me a chance to explain. If I could tell her the truth, everything would work out. She had to be willing to listen, though she may not be willing to do that anymore.

Lucy heard about my troubles and stopped in to visit me. I told her my story and she offered to help me. Julina hadn't been willing to take a letter from Paul, but she and Lucy were close friends. She'd certainly listen to Lucy. She agreed to visit her as soon as she could get to Emmaville. My heart soared. I hoped it wouldn't be too late.

Right after Lucy left, two men representing the English company owning the Emma visited me. I told the story over and over. Several times they asked if I had any idea where Shaun had hidden the mine production figures, but I didn't have a clue. The men told me they suspected the Emma had run into the fault several months before they bought it. My story verified that, but without the production figures they could prove nothing. They tried to talk to the other men working in the mine, but several key miners who would have known had disappeared.

The Englishmen excused themselves. They were on their way to talk to Katie Doherty.

The following morning, Florida finally arrived with Henry and a teenaged boy named Trace Rowe. The three of them walked over to Rico's cell. Rico, lying on his bunk, cursed. He told them to leave him alone. The boy and the two lawmen talked in hushed tones, and I heard the boy say, "That's him."

The jailor opened Rico's cell, and he was escorted down the hall to the next room. As they left, Henry Shields winked at me.

I got excited. I didn't know what he was planning, but I hoped they'd finally get Rico to talk. After several hours they returned. Rico entered his cell, and the jailer opened my cell door. "Pick up your things," he said. "You're free to go."

I let out a yip and jumped off the bunk. I grabbed Henry Shields and started dancing around the cell. He shoved me away and said, "You had better settle down, or I'll find some other reason to keep you here."

I stopped my dancing and said, "What happened?"

Henry smiled and walked out of my cell and over to Rico. "Rico confessed," he reported. Then, looking triumphantly at Rico, he said, "Hey Rico, the Rowe boy never seen you. We just made that story up. You swallowed the bait."

Rico leapt at the bars like an animal. He thrust his hands through the bars, clawing at Henry's throat, but Henry just stepped away. Rico cursed and spat at Henry. Henry backed up and walked up the hallway. Rico grabbed everything he could and threw it, but the bars made it impossible for him to throw accurately. As we closed the door to the jailhouse, I saw Rico beating his fists against the bars.

As soon as we were outside, I asked Henry, "What caused that?"

"After I left you," Henry explained, "I reasoned that Tex and his friends couldn't be as smart as they seemed. They must have slipped up someplace. On my way back to Alta, I stopped at the place where Rico found the sheriff's body. The first thing I noticed was how difficult the body would have been to find. The spot where he found the body came close to being a mile outside of Granite on the road to Sandy Station. The place the body had been hidden wasn't far from the road, but it lay behind a screen of scrub oak. The spot was marshy and crawling in stinging nettle.

"Even with Rico's careful description of the spot, I had a hell of a time finding it. No one would find that body unless they knew where it had been hidden.

"I noticed several small hills overlooking the site, and thought someone might have seen who had buried the sheriff. So I spread the word that if anyone had seen some men burying something near the seep on the Sandy Station Road, to let me know.

"No luck. So I went to Sheriff Florida with what I believed.

He listened and surprised me. He said, 'Henry, you really seem to believe that Stoner's innocent of the killing of Roderick. Do you really feel that way, or are you protecting him because he is your friend?'

"I replied, 'Sheriff, I'm convinced Stoner had nothing to do with any of these killings. It's true that Stoner is a good friend and I'd like to help him, but I have taken an oath to uphold the law. If I felt he was guilty, I wouldn't hesitate to see him tried.

"'His being involved in this mess makes no sense. You've already cleared him of the killing of Shaun. That means somebody must have planted the picture of Katie in his shack! And Stoner had nothing to gain by shooting the sheriff, but somebody in town did. Tex Hendricks.'

"I next told him all you'd told me, including Shaun having the mine production figures and Tex's attempt to get them."

"Florida said, 'Why haven't you told me this before?'

"'I haven't had any proof.'"

"'Do you think Rico killed Roderick?'"

"'I don't know,' I replied. 'I'm certain he was there when the sheriff was buried.'

"He said, 'If someone testified he saw Rico burying the sheriff, do you think he would talk to save his neck?'

"'I don't know, but I don't know any better way to get evidence against Tex.'

"Florida said, 'If we can't find a witness, we'd better make one.' He's the one who came up with the plan for the Rowe boy to be our witness. The plan called for him to identify Rico and watch for his response.

"When we walked Rico into this office, the Rowe boy told how he had been hunting. From the hillside he saw a Mexican drag something from a wagon and bury it. The boy left, and the marshal charged Rico with the murder of Sheriff Roderick."

Henry continued, "The marshal told Rico that the only way he could avoid the noose was to tell everything he knew. Rico panicked and took the hook. He told how he had nothing to do with the killing of the sheriff; his body had been loaded into the wagon the first time he saw it. Tex had shot the sheriff because he knew too much.

"The marshal wrote a statement and Rico signed it. Even then he had second thoughts, but he signed."

"What do we do now?" I asked.

"Since the body was found outside the jurisdiction of Alta City," he replied, "the federal marshal has taken responsibility. He drafted a warrant for the arrest of Tex; he and a few of his deputies are leaving immediately to arrest him. I brought your mare. You can ride with us."

I stepped outside as several deputies were saddling their horses and checking gear. As Henry led me to the horse he had brought, a carriage pulled up. Out of it stepped Lucy. As she approached, everyone stopped and stared. How must it be to get that kind of attention from men?

She walked up to me and said she had something for me. I told Henry to go on ahead, that I'd catch up. He and the others rode off, and I walked inside with Lucy. She handed me a letter and I read:

Dear Taw,

Lucy told me all that has happened to you since I last heard from you. I had not heard from you in some time. When I read in the papers that you were wanted for murder because of a fight over another man's wife, I was devastated. I didn't want to believe it, but I couldn't think that the papers would lie. I am so happy to hear that you are innocent. I should have had more faith in you.

I hope you can understand. At first I didn't believe the news of your shooting a man over another woman, but I listened to what Pa and Jed kept saying about you. You weren't around to talk to, and I had to make some decisions. I didn't hear from you for such a long time, and I faced a lot of pressure.

I am sorry Taw, but things have changed. I now see that I came to a hasty conclusion, but I don't think things can be the same between us. What I am trying to say is that I have accepted a marriage proposal from Jed. We're to be married in three days.

I don't know what to say. Please don't try to see me. It'll be too painful. I cannot change my mind now—all the preparations have been made. Forgive my lack of faith. I will always remember you fondly.

Love,

Julina

My head went back and my mouth fell open. I looked at Lucy. There were tears in her eyes. She reached out and gave me a hug. My mind went blank. I didn't know how to react. Should I be angry? Should I be more hurt? I stood in stunned silence.

Lucy, wiping the tears from her eyes, said, "What are you going to do, Taw?"

"I guess I'll go back to Alta and get my things. Then find some work."

"I could tell when I sat with Julina that she still loves you. She just doesn't think she can admit it. Go to her and make her tell you to your face that she doesn't love you anymore. If she can tell you to your face, then you will know that her feelings for you are dead." She wiped her eyes. "I would want to know that the man who loved me would fight to keep me."

"Should I go right now?" I asked.

"No," replied Lucy. "When I left there, she was planning to leave with her sisters to visit some friends, but she will be home tomorrow."

I gave Lucy a hug and thanked her for what she had done. She said, "I'll catch the train back to Wasatch tomorrow morning and stay at Lars' place for a few days."

I walked outside, jumped astride the sorrel mare, and set out for Alta.

Chapter Twenty-Two

The mare was a strong horse, but not fast. I primarily used her to pull the wagon, and she didn't get ridden often. Passing through Emmaville, I noticed several carriages and wagons out front of Orson Smith's place. I figured the wedding party must already be arriving. I didn't know what I would do once I reached Alta. I probably wouldn't be able to find work. The scandal about the Emma had scared investors in the other mines. At the same time, the U.S. Government had declared that silver dollars weren't going to be made any more.

The price of silver plummeted. Word spread that some of the smaller mines were going to close. It was ironic that as the railroad reached Alta, when mining should be the most profitable, the mines might close.

But that was the way of life in mining towns: one minute a miner faced the prospects of becoming richer than he could dream, the next minute he had to sneak out of town because he couldn't pay his bar tab.

I'd been lucky. Rather than gambling my money away or spending it on liquor, I'd given it to Lars to keep. Though we argued, he was the most honest man I knew. I had saved a sizeable chunk, and I owned several horses and a wagon. I could have a fresh start someplace else and begin a business, or I could buy some land and farm. The course I was going to choose depended on what Julina said when I saw her.

By the time I reached Alta, the posse had already been there. Someone probably saw it and telegraphed Tex that Sheriff Florida was coming to get him. Several men in town said Tex had lit out just before Florida arrived. He had taken the trail either through Grizzly Gulch or over Catherine Pass. The posse split up and went through both routes trying to find him.

I wandered over to the New Orleans Restaurant for dinner. Business had been bad lately. Repercussions from the Emma scandal were being felt everywhere. Only two other people besides me ate in the place that night. After dinner I wandered around town, stopping in several saloons and restaurants looking for work. Many familiar faces were gone. None of the businesses were busy.

Everywhere I went, the comments were the same: what little work there was had already been grabbed up. There were dozens of men like myself wandering around town, trying to find something to keep them busy. I decided I'd collect on the few debts people owed me, then pack up and head to Emmaville. I'd talk to Julina and then decide where my future lay.

A man who owed me money was broke. He gave me a pack frame to clear the debt. I had small accounts outstanding at the dry goods store and the livery stable. I remembered that I had left some clothes at Sam Gee's Laundry, so I dropped by to pick them up.

I paid for the clothes and went back to my shack to pack my things. While sitting in my bunk that night, I thought about several things, among them the biggest question of all: If Julina didn't marry me, was I going to keep going to church?

If I'd had the same viewpoint as when I was a boy, I would have blamed the Church for all my troubles. I would have reasoned that since I had started going to church, and had tried to do the right things, I shouldn't have been blamed for the murders, gotten shot, sat in jail, and lost my sweetheart. I would have felt that since I tried to do what was right, I should not have had any problems.

But I could see beyond that now. I had some faith. I had a different kind of understanding. I'd prayed, and I knew somebody was listening. I couldn't expect that I wouldn't have any more troubles, but I could count on not being alone when I searched for the answers. Still, I needed to straighten out something. I needed to talk to Lars.

I awoke early the next morning and packed my belongings on the back of the mare. Paul had come to town earlier and had taken my team, wagon, and all the harnesses down to Emmaville. He'd also taken my guns. I almost felt naked without them nearby, but I figured that Tex and his bunch must either be caught or out of the territory by now. I decided to have my last breakfast in Alta at Joe Brandy's place.

I took a seat inside facing the front door and near the far end of the bar. The bar ran along the left side of the room all the way to the window overlooking the street. The door opened on the right side of the room opposite the bar. I was preparing to dive into hot steaming cottage potatoes and eggs when I looked up, and to my horror saw Tex pass in front of the window. He entered the restaurant.

Seeing me, Tex shouted, "Stoner! You're dead!" Then he opened fire.

Expecting the worst, I dove behind the bar as he stepped through the door. He opened up, but not being able to see me, he shot randomly through the bar. Bullets were flying every-where as I crawled the length of the bar. Splinters showered me, and I felt the percussion of a slug that tore a hole inches from my face.

How he managed to miss, I cannot say. Taking a desperate chance, I reached for the ancient shotgun the bartender kept. At any minute, one of those slugs was going to have my initials on it. I heard Tex changing cylinders in his pistol. He was still standing in the doorway.

I jumped to my feet, shouting, "Hold it, Tex!" while at the same time lifting the shotgun. As I leveled the gun, it struck the bar sharply. The stock must have been rotten, because when I struck the bar, to my horror, the barrel fell off.

I was standing pointing the broken-off stock at Tex. He just smiled, showing his yellow teeth, and snapped the cylinder in place.

I took two steps, leaped through the window, and crashed into the boardwalk. As I tried to get to my feet, a board gave way and my right leg broke through. I did a one-legger into the hole.

I tried to pull my leg out, but the broken ends of the board painfully bit into my leg. I reached frantically into the hole, trying to push the boards away. Just then a pistol exploded, and a ball smashed into the boardwalk next to me. I turned and looked into Tex's evil face. He grinned and worked the tobacco in his cheek. The pistol bucked again, and the wood under my hand exploded into splinters. My heart skipped a beat. Again he had deliberately missed. He was toying with me. I didn't think he was going to miss again.

His grin widened, and his yellow teeth and black gums made me sick. He said, "Stoner, you've been troublesome to me. I'm going to take a lot of pleasure in watching you . . . ."

I saw a streak of dark metal sweep toward Tex. The blade of a shovel slammed Tex into the wall. His pistol flew out of his hand and skidded along the boardwalk, dropping off the edge. Looming where Tex had stood was Lars. Cocking the shovel, he swung again. Smashing across Tex's chest, the shovel handle cracked and splintered in half. Tex swore, and his head whipped back into the wall. He dropped to one knee, then seemed to be reaching for another gun. Lars bellowed, reached down, lifted Tex up, and slammed him to the boardwalk. Tex gasped and went limp. Lars searched him. He found a derringer in his belt and a pistol in his right boot. Lars tossed the guns aside, then dragged Tex off the boardwalk and into the street.

Several horses pounded up the street and slid to a stop. Henry Shields stepped off his sorrel gelding. Tex began to stir. Shields roughly turned him on his face and locked cuffs onto his wrists. The deputies jerked him to his feet and dragged him toward the jailhouse.

I was able to work my leg loose and pulled it from the hole. Lars stepped to me and asked in his heavy accent, "Have you been shot? Are you all right?"

I nodded. He put his hands out, grabbing me by the shoulders. Looking me in the eyes, he said, "Are you sure, son?"

"He never hit me. He was playing with me. If you hadn't come when you did . . . I wouldn't be talking."

He pulled me close, and his mighty arms hugged me so tight I thought I was going to pass out. "Paul told me you'd been cleared and gone back to Alta. I was chopping wood near Wasatch when a rider told me Tex had just ridden through town heading back to Alta. I had to warn you. I jumped on my horse and got here as quick as I could. I . . . I was so worried I'd get here too late." His voice cracked.

A lump formed in my throat. It had been almost ten years since I'd first seen him, and he'd changed very little. His short hair had a few flecks of gray and his neck was thicker, but he was still as powerful as a grizzly bear.

Lars continued, "I'm so glad you're all right."

Then I did something I'd never done before. I hugged him back, and the words came. "Lars, I've treated you bad. Most of our fights were because I was doing things just to get under your skin. I can't say I even know why I done those things."

Lars tried to interrupt, but I cut him off. "You got to let me finish this or I'll never get it out. You tried to be a pa to me. You treated me fair, but I wouldn't let you get close." In a quiet voice I continued, "I'm sorry, and . . . and . . . I love you, Lars." I couldn't believe it. I'd said it. I never thought I could get those words out.

Lars' eyes glistened. He couldn't speak. He gave me a hug that felt like he'd crushed my spine.

Chapter Twenty-Three

Henry had been riding down Grizzly Flat Trail when he had heard gunshots. He supposed Tex might try to sneak back into town. He had paused on a ridge just above town when he saw the drama unfold on the boardwalk in front of Brandy's place. He put the spurs to his mount. By the time he reached town, Lars had Tex down in the street.

Henry spoke. "Lars, could you get over to the telegraph office and wire Silver Fork? Let them know we got Tex in jail. Might as well wire the folks in Granite and Sandy, too." Lars waved good-bye and stepped astride his big draft horse.

Jumping through the window and landing on the glass had given me several deep cuts. Henry sent for the doctor, and he stitched me up. It took a few hours, and I was antsy to get on and see Julina. Then Sheriff Florida rode in, and he made me tell him the story over and over again before he let me leave town.

I was finally able to get on my horse and head down the canyon. I was worn out and sore when I approached the Smiths' place. The sun played peek-a-boo with me between the peaks to the west. I entered the yard and was approaching the house when two men stepped out from between some carriages and asked what I wanted.

I replied, "I just came to call."

One of the men said, "You're going to have to do better than that, stranger. Killers are on the run from Alta; how do we know you ain't one of them?"

I said in a surly voice, "Your killer's been caught this morning. So if you'd get out of the way, I'll see Julina."

The two men looked at each other, and one whispered, "Stoner." The other said, "Wait."

He disappeared into the house. In a moment he returned with Jed. Two of his brothers followed him. "Get out of here, Stoner, and leave my wife alone."

I replied, "She ain't your wife yet."

"As far as you are concerned she is. Besides, she don't want to see you."

"Fine, let her tell me that," I said.

I dismounted and tried to push my way past him. He jumped into my path and said, "Stoner, haven't I given you enough beatings to knock some sense into your thick skull? Aren't you smart enough to see that you've been beaten by a better man? Get out of here now, or me and my brothers will be glad to give you one last whopping."

"Jed, the only reason you can get away with saying that is that you have lots of help. Any time and any place I'll take you on, but not with your brothers holding me so I can't hit back. I'm not afraid of a fair fight. What about you?"

The veins popped out on his neck and he jumped towards me. I shoved him hard. One of his brothers grabbed his shoulder and said, "Not here, later." He turned to me and shouted, "Get! Or I'll have to say you pulled a gun and I had to shoot you in self-defense."

"That'll be some story. I'm not carrying a gun." I wanted to put my fist in each of their mouths. They'd all back him with whatever story he wanted told. If there was trouble, I'd get thrown in jail.

I turned, leaped on the mare, and spun around. Jed whispered to his brothers. I put my heels to the mare and thundered out of the yard.

I didn't know what to do, but I wanted to talk to somebody so I lit out for Granite to find Paul. About halfway there, I met Paul and Deputy Shields coming the opposite direction. I began to tell them what had happened at the Smiths' place. Suddenly all our horses' ears pricked, and they turned their heads in the direction I had just come. I turned my mare and she walked a few steps forward. It was just dark enough that Paul and Deputy Shields,who were standing in the shadow of an oak, were almost invisible.

My mare stood, ears pricked, looking back down the road I'd just ridden over. Several riders were charging at a full run, and a fair guess would be that they weren't planning on being friendly. The sun had settled below the hills, but I could make out five. Jed was in the lead. It didn't surprise me! He was coming to teach me a lesson when he thought I'd be alone.

Jed was in for a surprise.

As he thundered up, he leaned back and slid his big horse to a stop. It was all the others could do to keep from running over the top of him.

One of them snatched at my bridle. Nate and Seth leapt from their horses and wrestled me off my mare.

I hardly put up a fight, but Jed didn't seem to notice. His brothers were big farm boys whose shoulders were so wide they'd fill a doorway. Jed, on the other hand, was almost as tall but more slender. He was the pretty boy of the bunch—the one all the gals wanted to dance with.

After I'd been yanked from my horse, they held me. Jed taunted, "Taw Stoner, you talked real big back at the Smith place. You tried to make me look like a fool in front of my gal. I'd have thought that after all the whuppins I give ya, you'd be smart enough to stay out of my way. Guess your momma never raised any bright children.

"Well, you're not going to need to be smart to remember the beating you're going to get now. You won't ever forget this one. Hold him, boys. Stew! Throw me that bull whip."

Jed reached for the whip, and I saw wicked delight flash in his eyes as he stepped back. He snapped the whip easily. It cracked like a squirrel rifle. Jed's brothers stretched me between them with my back towards Jed. The whip popped above my head. "Next one's for you," Jed cackled with glee.

From the shadows came the twin sounds of hammers being cocked. In one motion, Jed and his brothers turned and saw Deputy Henry Shields and my step-brother Paul astride their mounts under the branches of scrub oak. Jed and his brothers had ridden past them when they charged up.

Shields shouted, "We've seen enough. Jed, you talk pretty big when ya got 'em held down and outnumbered. I reckon ya might not talk so big if ya had to face Taw like a man." He rolled a wad of tobacco in his cheek and spat in the dust. "Sounds like I might have ta put the lot of ya in jail. But I ain't in no hurry, and I've always been partial to fistfights. Since you're so eager ta teach 'em a lesson, unbuckle and throw down that whip. Then let's see what you can do with them fists—not yer mouth. Have a problem with that, Taw?"

"Not a one," I answered with a smile.

Pointing to the others, Henry said, "Ya back away now, boys . . . don't even think about jumping in. Jailhouse in Alta's hardly been used this summer. Sure you boys could break it in real nice."

I'd jerked away from Jed's brothers; glaring, they stepped back slowly. It was rapidly becoming dark, but I could see the blood drain from Jed's sour face. He stood stunned-like—didn't move. I reached out with my foot and kicked the whip from his hand. Paul had jumped from his horse and pulled the pistol from his holster.

I'd waited years for a chance to face Jed with none of his brothers to step in. I smiled as I thought what must be going through his head. Last thing Jed wanted was to fight without somebody holding me. He'd always talked big when he had a backup, but now it was him and me.

But suddenly, all the hate that had built up in me over the

years drained away. I was finally going to have an even chance with Jed; but in spite of all the things he'd done, I no longer had the desire for revenge. Instead, I felt sorry for him. He was so unsure of himself that he was forced to live hiding behind the people around him. It was just a matter of time before everyone him saw him for what he was.

I spoke. "Jed, get on your horse and get out of here. This won't change nothing. There's no sense in you getting whupped."

I could see that his mind was racing. Then the shocked look left his face. He squared his jaw, glared at me and snarled, "Stoner, you haven't got it in you to whup me."

With that he began rolling his sleeves. That gave me a start. He wasn't the coward I'd expected. "Jed," I reasoned, "I don't have any desire to fight anymore. You ain't worth it. I'm giving you a chance."

Jed snarled like a mountain lion and charged. He wildly threw his fists at me; I easily dodged them, stepping to the side. I put up my fists to ward off his blows and tried to reason with him. "How's it going to look, you showing up to get hitched all beat up? Walk away. You can end this now. Why, you can even tell everyone you whupped me. I won't say any different."

That must have been the wrong thing to say, because he bellowed and charged again. As he came in, I slipped a jab to his mouth. It snapped his head and set him back on his heels. A shocked look came to his face. He wiped the blood from his mouth.

Then a new determination came to him. I saw it in his eyes. I saw it in the way he held his chin. I was in this fight until one of us couldn't get up.

He began to circle, keeping out of reach. He was measuring me, scouting for a weakness. When he thought he'd got me figured out, he'd come. He wasn't going to be the pushover I'd thought.

He flashed several jabs to my face. A few missed and a couple grazed me. I countered, but was a might slow. He guessed my moves and kept away. Somebody had shown him how to box. He'd overcome his initial rage and was waiting for his best chance. The circling got me antsy. I ached to charge in and mix it up, but I was wary. I'd seen enough fights to know that eventually he'd make a mistake.

Jed continued to jab and dance. I pressed forward, cutting off his escape routes.

In all our previous battles, his brothers had always held me. I'd never had an even break, so he hadn't seen what I could do with my fists. Years of hard work had made me powerful and strong. I wasn't fancy, able to slip punches or dance out of reach. But I could take a punch and dish out more than my share.

I was sure I could take the best that Jed could throw. I doubted he could take mine.

I threw a right that he ducked, but my fist grazed his cheekbone. Foolishly, I charged in. He stepped aside and peppered me with punches. A jab fattened my lip. Another bloodied my nose. We separated. I'd gotten the worst of that exchange. I'd have to be more careful. He was dangerous.

He continued to jab. My face was covered with welts and bruises. He'd keep this up forever unless I baited him. I'd have to set him up and counter punch. I stepped forward, feinting with my left. He dodged right and I anticipated. My right hook caught him in the ear and snapped his head. He slipped my left, but another right crashed into his ribs. He gasped and staggered backwards, sitting in the dust.

He was shocked. I'd caught him by surprise. I moved in, planning to let him have it as soon as he stood up. He leapt to his feet and threw a fist full of dust into my face. I tried to cover and he saw an opening. He came at me with a left, another left, and a right to my ribs. I staggered backwards, but he pressed forward, peppering me to the midsection.

As he pulled away, I dropped my arms around him and drove him into the ground. The collision jarred us both. My head smashed into his mouth and he cursed. He smashed an elbow to my throat and pulled free.

Jed staggered to his feet. I was slower and he rushed at me, aiming a wicked kick to my face. I blocked it, but he sent a shot to my chin that had me seeing stars. As I rose to my feet he connected several other times, but I was too groggy to remember where. I covered as best I could. I blocked some, but he closed my eye and split my cheek.

He clearly had the upper hand, and I had to do something before he connected with a punch that would finish me. I baited him by dropping my right hand. He saw it and threw a roundhouse left. I jumped to the side and connected with a solid right to his jaw.

His knees buckled, but he caught himself. I pressed forward with a stream of punches, most of them connecting. A left snapped his head. Another left put him on his heels, and a right crashed into his stomach, doubling him over. I measured him and sent a right onto the point of his chin. His head snapped back and he dropped like a sack of potatoes.

He lay on the ground and didn't move. It was too dark to see his face, but I could tell he was out. His brothers dumped a canteen over his head, and after some coaxing sat him up. They lifted him. He staggered to his horse, and they helped him into his saddle. He leaned forward and wrapped both arms around the neck of his horse. His face was dark, but I could see blood dripping from his chin.

Henry smiled and spat tobacco juice in the dirt. "Boys," he said, "it was a fair fight. If I hear you've been spreading word any different, I just might have to haul you in for a week or two on a drunk and disorderly."

The men slapped their horses and jogged back towards the Smiths'. I should have felt good about myself, but I didn't. I hadn't wanted to fight, but I'd been forced into it. Even though I'd beaten him, Jed had won. The story would be twisted so it would look like I'd bullied him. Jed would use it to turn Julina against me. Any chance that I might have had of speaking to her would be gone. Jed had Julina, and I saw no way I could get her back.

I guess I should have felt bad about Jed taking his wedding vows with black eyes and big swollen lips. But I didn't. I guess a pious person would. I wasn't that perfect yet.

We turned our horses towards Emmaville and soon arrived at Lars' place. Paul and Henry had business elsewhere and left me alone in the barn.

I rubbed my horse down, gave her some grain, and checked myself over. My knuckles were scraped and I had a cut on my cheek. My face was puffy, but after rinsing it with cold water I looked presentable.

I walked over to an old crate and sat down, feeling sorry for myself. I said a quiet prayer. I said I wanted more than anything to marry Julina. Regardless of what happened, I had changed and was going to live differently. I then asked that things would work out so I could marry Julina.

By the time I finished, I felt peaceful and hopeful. While pondering, I heard a noise. To my surprise, Lucy walked in. I told her everything. Short of riding up with my gun drawn, I had no idea how I'd see Julina.

"Are you going to give up, Taw?"

"What can I do, Lucy? There's no way I'll be able to get past Jed and his brothers. After the whuppin I gave him, he'll have a poster out for my arrest."

Lucy looked at me from under her long lashes and said, "I think I can get her away from the house for a short while tomorrow morning. Go and wait near the cottonwood grove on Willow Creek. I'll bring her by. Then you'll have to turn on your charm, little brother."

I grabbed her and kissed her on the cheek.

All night long I tossed and turned, thinking about seeing Julina. I was up before dawn, too nervous to eat. I left without breakfast.

I rode without direction. While riding, I practiced what I was going to say. It never sounded right.

Lucy took several of her friends to the Smiths' place. She was going to make some excuse about the girls getting together for last-minute advice.

My riding brought me to Willow Creek. I ground hitched the mare. She hung her head and swatted flies with her tail. My throat was dry and my palms wet. It was like waiting to be hanged. It seemed like three lifetimes, but I finally heard the girls approaching. I promptly forgot everything I had planned to say and stood with a lump in my throat, feeling an urge to run. I stepped behind a tree. I needed to be certain that Jed hadn't followed. The group approached, laughing. I waited until the last moment and stepped out.

My sudden appearance startled a couple of the young women, and when Julina turned her head and saw me, she had a pained look in her eyes. She said in a low voice, "Oh, Taw."

She was even prettier than the last time I saw her. We stood and looked at each other for a long time. Neither of us spoke or moved. Tears filled her eyes, and she turned her back towards me.

I stepped closer and said, "I've been practicing what I'd say ever since Lucy brought me that letter. I even wrote it down so I wouldn't forget. Now, standing here looking at you, none of those words sound good enough."

"It's too late for us, Taw. I'll be married tomorrow. Arrangements have been made. People have come a long way. I can't let them down."

"That's not you talking, that's Jed and your pa. Are they going to live your life? Are you going to marry Jed because it will make you happy, or everyone else?"

She gave me an angry look and said, "My whole family is up in arms over the beating you gave Jed. He lost several teeth, and his face is so swollen I hardly recognize him. How could you do that?"

"Jed followed me out of your yard with a couple of his brothers, intending to use his bullwhip on me," I explained. "They caught up and were holding me so Jed could whip me. Then Henry Shields stepped in and made the others let me go. For once in his life, Jed was in a fair fight. I gave him a chance to leave. He's the one who pressed the fight. You saw how he fared."

I stepped closer, reached out, and grabbed her shoulders. She stiffened. "Julina, if you really care for him more than for me, then I'll leave and you'll never see me again. But if you don't, you'll never find happiness with Jed."

"Your father means well. He wants you to marry someone who will provide for you and your children. But do you really think he'll insist upon you marrying someone who won't bring you happiness?"

I could feel her sobbing and I said, "Yesterday, a man chased me and tried to kill me. I was trapped. He was holding a loaded gun. I would much rather face that killer and his loaded gun than face the thought of losing you. What I fear more than anything is that I'll never be able to be with you again."

"I want more than anything to be your husband. I've even decided I would become a churchgoing man. I'll wait here until noon tomorrow. If you don't come, I'll know you love Jed more. I'll ride away and you won't have to think about me anymore, but I hope you'll come. I don't want to lose you. More than anything, I want you to be happy. If Jed is the man who'll do that for you, then . . . ." I started to choke up. I didn't know if I could continue.

She turned and faced me while wiping her tears away with the back of her hands. I gave her my scarf. She looked into my eyes. Then I said, "In case I never see you again, I have to kiss you just one more time."

I pulled her close. She was stiff and didn't respond. As my lips touched hers, her arms stayed at her side. It must really be over between us. My heart sank. I began to pull away, when suddenly she relaxed and threw her arms around my neck. We kissed and I held her, feeling her heart racing. I didn't want to let go, but she began to pull away. As she did, I whispered, "Tomorrow at noon. I'll wait until then. I love you, Julina." She gave my hand a squeeze and reluctantly walked away.

I watched her go. She looked back twice before disappearing.

I was hopeful, sad, worried, and happy, all at the same time. My future was out of my control. It now rested in the hands of a lovely girl with beautiful green eyes.

I walked my horse back to Lars', but I didn't want to see anyone. I put some food together, found my bedroll, and rode off. I felt anxious, but there was nothing else I could do. I don't remember the trail I took, but I found myself high on the mountainside above Emmaville by that evening. I decided to make a camp and sleep on the mountain.

A dozen times that night I dreamed that Julina ran to me in the meadow; a dozen more times I waited all afternoon and rode off alone. Before dawn, I rode down the mountain. I got all my gear, supplies, and guns together, then took some of the money I had saved and wrote a note to Lars, telling him I'd telegraph when I needed the rest.

Several towns were experiencing mining booms. Jerico and Park City were still mining. I could go to any of those places and find work. I wanted to believe Julina would meet me in the meadow, but deep down I knew this only happened in story-books.

I mounted my horse and started him toward the cottonwood grove on Willow Creek. Once there, I reined in and slid down off his big back.

The small creek whispered as it wound its way through the field of sun-dried grass. Along its banks, hungry trout dimpled the surface film in search of insects fallen from the overhanging bank. Nearby, robins kicked through the patches of grass and dead leaves, searching for hoppers that were too chilled from the night air to escape their darting beaks.

The tall mountains to the east kept the warming sunlight off this small meadow for a spell, but far to the west, the morning sun was already warming the peaks of the Oquirrhs. Next to me stood a lonely cottonwood tree. It had stood so long that the chattering birds and busy squirrels seemed to take no notice of it at all. If lightning were to strike it down, I wondered if the animals would pause to notice its passing. I felt like that tree as

I sat watching the world waking around me. If Julina didn't come to the meadow, I would ride off, never returning. Would anyone notice that I had gone?

In a few hours, I'd know. If she became Jed's wife, I'd ride away from this valley forever. "She's not going to tell me I have to leave," I thought to myself, "but if she doesn't walk into this meadow by noon, I'm going to step into the saddle and take the quickest trail out of here. I could never stand to see Julina the wife of another man."

I spent the morning alone with my hopes and fears. I watched the sun rise, the shadows shrink and begin to lengthen. With each passing moment, my hope for being with Julina faded. I tried to deny her decision, but as the hours passed I couldn't any longer. It was well past noon and she hadn't come. "Julina has chosen Jed over me." Just saying it was almost more than I could stand.

I checked my gear, making sure it was still tied tight. I looked at the mountains to the east. I sighed, then placed my hand on the worn saddle horn. "Oh, Julina," I said aloud, "you'll never know how much I'm going to miss you."

I began to speak more, but started to choke up. I placed my left foot awkwardly in the stirrup and tried to swing my leg over the back of the horse.

A white hand was grasping my ankle. I spun from the saddle and dropped to the ground. Julina stood there, and I was looking into the prettiest pair of green eyes I'd ever seen in my life.

She stepped close and whispered, "Did you mean what you said yesterday?"

I could hardly talk. My heart was racing. I had just gone from the depths of despair to soaring with happiness in a few seconds. Somehow I managed to squeak out, "Every word."

Julina smiled, and her dimples showed. "Jed and his family left early this morning. There hasn't been enough time to get the word out that the wedding is off. The guests will be arriving at Pa's house soon."

"Well, everyone expects a wedding," I replied. "Let's not disappoint them."

With that I pulled her close. We kissed for the longest time.

NOTES

The entire truth about early Alta will probably never be known. Elements of truth have become so mixed with fantasy that the two cannot be distinguished easily. The Englishmen who bought the Emma continued to scream fraud, but nothing was ever proved. Within a few months the newspapers found other scandals to report, and the Emma was forgotten.

During the peak of Alta's boom, it is not really known how many people lived there. Several have suggested that there were between 5,000 and 8,000 inhabitants. However, that number couldn't have possibly lived in the small valley during the years of 1872 and 1873. There simply weren't enough mining jobs to support so many.

The Emma and the Flagstaff employed seventy or more miners each. Three or four mines employed twelve to twenty miners. The remaining mines employed two to four miners. The total number of active mines never reached more than forty during the peak years of silver production. A large number of individuals were prospecting on their own, but to support the kind of population mentioned above, prospectors would have to be working shoulder to shoulder on the open hillsides. In reality, the maximum number of inhabitants probably never exceeded 2,000.

Two saloons, the Gold Miner's Daughter and the Bucket of Blood, are credited for being the places where between 100 and 150 people were killed in gunfights. Yet no mention of those two saloons can be found during the boom years of Alta. It's probable that these two saloons came into existence after the boom years.

Were stories of so many killed in gunfights exaggerated? More than likely. Did many gunfights occur in the Gold Miner's Daughter and the Bucket of Blood? Probably not. These saloons probably received this reputation because of their colorful names, and also due to the fact that they both were still standing in the

1930s—two of the last buildings of old Alta to exist.

Yet many of the romantic stories regarding Alta likely had their basis in fact. The author has intertwined his story with early tales about Alta. For example, the story about the itinerant drunk who claimed to resurrect the dead has been quoted by several sources.

The intent of the author has been to be as historically accurate as possible. Every business named existed at the time of the story.

Alta came into existence around the year 1868. At first its primary business was lumbering, but with the coming of the railroad in 1869, ore could be transported at a reasonable expense. The growth became explosive over the next couple of years as hoards of men and women swarmed to Alta, spurred on by dreams of instant wealth just waiting to be found. The town grew so quickly that a small nearby town, Central City, was swallowed up by the human tide of prospectors and miners.

Like most such towns in the West, more money was probably made and lost by the big-time investors buying and selling stock than was ever dug from the ground. In late 1873, the bubble burst. The Emma scandal, demonitorization of the silver dollar, and land ownership disputes caused people to seek for riches elsewhere.

Through the remainder of the 1870s and 1880s, fires and avalanches destroyed bits and pieces of the town; and each time, less was rebuilt than had been destroyed. Then in 1885, a major avalanche destroyed most of the town, and Alta was left to decay. Like a relic stored on a shelf, she gathered dust and was forgotten. In the early 1900s, with the rise in the price of silver, a resurgence occurred for a few years; but the "Old West" flavor of Alta had died.

Today, an old cemetery lies at the foot of a popular ski run. Not a headstone or grave marker exists anywhere to prove its existence, but the ski patrol knows it's there. Sometimes early in the morning after a heavy snowfall, long before the lifts open, a ski patrolman will find a single set of ski tracks through the snow. Can ghosts resist the greatest snow on earth?

The basement of the current Snow Pine Lodge is built over the old general store. The opening to the Emma mine is on the north side of the canyon, and most residents can point to its location. Attempts have been made to close off all old mine openings, but in some cases care must be taken so that a skier doesn't fall into some forgotten shaft.

Emmaville was later moved and renamed Ragtown. This move merely prolonged the inevitable, and the town soon died. Nothing but a few stone foundations remain of the towns of Tanner, Granite, Silver Fork, and Wasatch. A hundred years from now, even their memory may be lost.

As with many of the towns of the Old West, perhaps it is better that we never know the entire truth about Alta. In fact, its greatest charm may be the compelling uncertainty that adds so much mystique and romance to its history.

About the Author

A loan officer in a California mortgage company, Rob Robles goes home from work and changes into a historian who is in love with the wild, wild west. That affection is apparent in his first novel, *The Claim*.

Rob and his wife, Jeane, and their six children love the outdoors, horseback riding, fly fishing, and being together. They live in Morgan Hill, a suburb of San Jose.